The Recruit's Handbook

Andrew Hill

Copyright © 2020 Andrew Hill
All rights reserved.
ISBN: 978-1-65966-107-1

DEDICATION

This book is dedicated to all high school student-athletes who embrace the counter-cultural reality of sports: you have to pay the price just to get a shot at being successful. It is a journey of faith and self-discovery. Who you become in the process is more valuable that what you achieve from it. To all of my former, current, and future athletes, THANK YOU for the privilege of being your coach. And to all student-athletes looking to play in college, I wish you the best of luck and success. I hope this book can shed some light on the confusing and chaotic world of recruiting.

CONTENTS

	Introduction	1
1	Self-Inventory: Is College Athletics for Me?	4
2	Levels of Play	22
3	Being a College Athlete	29
4	Myths & Misunderstandings	35
5	Snakes: Recruiting Services	48
6	Eligibility Requirements	57
7	The Academic Plan	67
8	The Timeline	73
9	Promoting Yourself to College Coaches	82
10	College Visits	94
11	Recruiting Violations	99
12	Commitment, Signing, & the NLI	102
13	Transitioning to College	109
	Epilogue	114

ACKNOWLEDGMENTS

I am very blessed to have a loving family led by a supportive wife, Kate. Thank you for all that you do for us. Thank you to my mother who gave me a love of writing, and also serves as my chief editor. I am grateful to all of my former and current players that have trusted me in the recruiting process. And I am thankful for a supportive coaching staff and administration. Finally, I have to gratefully acknowledge all of the college coaches with whom I have worked with over my career. Your insight into this process, along with your annual interest in our student-athletes, has provided much of the framework we use in the recruiting process.

INTRODUCTION

This book was written for high school student-athletes and parents who are interested in the possibility of playing a sport at the collegiate level. For many young people, the hundreds (or thousands) of hours invested in honing one's skills and the process of falling in love with the game creates this desire to continue playing at the next level. Even when one has both the skill and desire to play in college, the process can be chaotic and confusing at best. The purpose of this book is to equip you with the proper perspectives, pertinent information, and a road map for pursuing the opportunity to play your sport at the collegiate level.

There is no doubt that the allure of college athletics can be intoxicating. Our society has morphed into a constant stream of promotion (often self-promotion) and excitement around athletics, and collegiate competition holds significant prestige and value. ESPN will air it's National Signing Day specials just to track where the top high school football and basketball players will continue to play in college. However, collegiate athletics is so much more than the initial splash of a five-star athlete choosing a high profile school. The truth is that most high school athletes are not five-star recruits, and that the recruiting process will take many twists and turns, far outside the reach of ESPN's coverage. This book is aimed at the 99.9% of high school athletes whose college decision will not be broadcast nationally.

Athletic involvement, much like in high school, can enhance your experience in college both from the competitive environment to the relationships that form as a result of your involvement. While the sport itself is something that you have grown to know and love, moving from the high school level to the college level is a new experience. The game you love simultaneously stays the same but drastically changes. Athletes enter college as a teenager and are competing for positions and playing time against young adults. Terminology changes. Coaching styles – and sometimes entire coaching staffs – change and often come with a different feeling. When scholarships are involved, the expectations can lead an athlete to feel greater obligation to the team/sport than to receiving an education. All in all, this is a very different, yet rewarding, experience within your sport. After finishing this book, you will have a better understanding of what to expect when you get to your college team. When you know what to expect, you will be better positioned to be successful and feel connected early in your college career.

One staple of the recruiting process, and which is true for pretty much every sport, is the chaotic and sometimes irrational nature of recruiting. I have seen clear Division I athletes be passed over to become All-Americans at Division II or Division III. At the same time, I've seen less capable athletes be given scholarship opportunities that never translate into athletic success on the field/court. I've seen schools walk into my building two months after the signing date with a scholarship offer for a player who stayed patient in the process, and I've seen an FBS (football, Division I) coach brought to tears as he explains to a worthy athlete how there are no more offers available. This process is chaotic, unfair, competitive, and often involves a narrow focus and stereotypical evaluation. Yet, the more you are aware of the various aspects that are involved with playing college sports and the recruiting process, the more empowered you will be as you start your journey.

I am a high school teacher (Social Studies, primarily Psychology) and Head Football Coach at Woodbury High School (MN). Throughout my 21-year coaching career I have coached baseball, softball, basketball (Boys & Girls), and golf. I have counseled many student-athletes (football and otherwise) during the recruiting process, and each year I speak many times about this process. My perspective is that of a high school coach who has helped dozens of student-athletes connect with the opportunity to continue their careers. Within my football program, we have a detailed process through which we help guide our student-athletes to collegiate opportunities. In fact, athletes from neighboring schools (and other programs within my school) will reach out each year for assistance in their own navigation of the recruiting process.

I am confident in what we do, and my experiences within the recruiting process has led me to write this book. Outside of the publishing of this book, I do not have a financial investment in "selling" recruiting services – there is no subscription or service that I am trying to solicit. In fact, later in this book I will make an air tight case for NEVER using a paid recruiting service. Ultimately, helping student-athletes and their parents find confidence within the recruiting process will benefit the athlete, their family, their high school team, and their school. And this will help improve the overall state of high school sports in general. Therefore, I firmly believe that this will be both informative and enjoyable, and ultimately that this book will provide a sense of calm amidst the chaos of the recruiting process.

1 SELF-INVENTORY
IS COLLEGE ATHLETICS FOR ME?

It is critically important as we start this journey for each student-athlete to take time to honestly evaluate the questions within this chapter. If you are a parent reading this chapter, I suggest that you give these questions to your son or daughter, and give him or her ample time to think through each question and answer honestly. Then bring the answers back to a discussion as a family (if this is your family's process). If you are an individual athlete reading this, I strongly recommend taking the time - even if it's a few days – to process and answer these questions **BEFORE proceeding with this book.** The only wrong answer to these questions is an inauthentic answer. And it's perfectly fine to be unsure of an answer, but it is important to start to process each question.

Readers beware – if you think the point of this book is to make an argument for every reader (or child of a parent reader) to hard charge into collegiate athletics, you are mistaken. I love high school sports. I love college sports. And, I love connecting high school athletes with meaningful opportunities to play sports in college. But I also have a deep respect for athletes who know themselves and realize that when their high school career ends, their athletic career may end or take a back seat at the same time. Student-athletes are not failures if they choose to not continue their sport in college. The group that I feel the saddest for is the student-athletes who feel they must continue in college, only to find themselves in a less than ideal situation where their once beloved athletic careers die a slow death. Thus, the purpose of this chapter is to have the student-athlete, himself or herself, examine whether the pursuit of playing in college is the right path.

Questions to consider:

- What do I love about my sport?
- Why do I want to play my sport in college?
- What am I looking for in a college outside of my sport?
- What are the geographical parameters for college?
- What do I want to do after college? Does this influence my playing sports?
- What financial considerations are needed in selecting a college?
- What are my training habits in regards to my sport?
- How would my teammates and coach describe me?
- What are my participation expectations in my first year on campus?

What Do I Love About My Sport?

To lead off with this question seems easy, but it cuts to the heart of the pursuit of playing your sport in college. There is no specific answer that should point you towards playing or not playing in college, but rather you want to be looking at whether or not your "driving force" that has driven you to play in high school will be present in college. And if it is not present in college, will there be a different but powerful source of motivation that will drive you to be successful at the next level?

For example, often times in high school, senior athletes will remark about how special it was to play a sport they loved with their friends and teammates with whom they grew up. The sense of community has been fostered from a young age, and there is great pride in representing one's neighborhood, city, and/or community. This is a powerful motive, yet one that will not be as powerful as you move on to college. How quickly and how willing are you to form new friendships and relationships? If the sense of community is critical to you, how willing are you to invest in your new school and local community to create that sense of connection at your college? Are there factors in your potential schools that can help create this?

Or perhaps you love the adrenaline rush of competition. Sports often allow us to compete in ways that are difficult or frowned upon outside of the sport. Can you imagine a wrestler trying to take down the Starbucks barista for a fall? We cheer it within the context of a wrestling match, but probably call the police if we see it in public. This can be a powerful motive for many athletes – to challenge oneself in the arena of competition with another in our sport.

For many, the process of pursuing excellence within their sport has helped develop them as an individual outside of sports. This "falling in love with the process" is something that has expanded beyond your sport to other areas of your life. When you face adversity, you draw comparisons to the adversity you have overcome within your athletic career. You embrace new challenges because you believe they make you a better person. Please note, many people believe this to be true, but it might not be a strong motive or why you love your sport – it could be a positive side effect. As you continue to play in college, adversity will strike and you will be faced with new challenges, so the process will continue.

Many high school athletes love their sport because of who they are, or the social status they feel is associated with their sport. On the surface this sounds like vanity, and for some it is, but for others the motive of affiliation is strong. Many love being part of a team and being able to represent their school and community, and for being recognized outside of their sport. Others receive media recognition and this exchange of notoriety for athletic performance is desired. I don't include this with any judgment, and I'm not implying that it's selfish or bad. But the truth is that many athletes who increase in popularity because of their sport will tie their own self-image to their sports performance. Thus, they are driven to continue to participate because they are unsure of life outside of their sport.

Or perhaps, this question might lead you in an unexpected direction. Maybe the love of the sport has always been an external prop that you no longer desire to keep up. What you once thought was the love of the sport was simply trying to make Mom or Dad happy, and the end of high school might be a good time to conclude your career. Maybe you have tried to live up to a legacy of performance set by previous athletes, friends, or family members, and the step to college separates you from any shadow you operated under previously.

My hope in this is not to direct you towards not continuing in college, but I have seen a significant number of athletes end their careers only a few weeks into their college careers. Outside of injury, the number one reason that they cite is their "loss of the love of the game" upon entering the collegiate level. Thus, as you start your journey into the recruiting process, I think it is critically important to evaluate (a) what do you love about your sport, and (b) is it likely that what you love will be present, or interchangeable with something new, when you get to the next level?

Why Do I Want To Play In College?

Your answer to this could easily overlap with your answer from the previous question – if what you love about playing in high school is present in your opportunity to play collegiately, then that is a strong reason to continue playing. However, can you also objectively list some reasons why you want to play in college? I will outline some possible answers that might align you're your thoughts. You may have reasons outside of what I discuss. These first two questions really come down to your motivation for playing college sports – when the motivation is strong, the athlete's resolve is also strong. However, there are also some answers that can point you, in a time of honest reflection, to the fact that you might not have a strong motivation to continue playing.

For many who want to play in college, this desire stems from the habit of participation. Because you have played your sport for a number of years, and have found enjoyment and fulfillment from participating, you simply want to continue to play. This can be a strong motive. The habits that have led you to be successful in high school have established the basis for continued success in college (when combined with other areas of growth). While being an athlete does not define who you are, your participation is meaningful to you and you want to continue to have this be a part of your identity.

For others, participation in exchange for a scholarship may feel like a necessity. In this situation, the cost of attending college is too steep to cover without financial assistance, and the opportunity to earn a scholarship tied to athletic involvement provides an opportunity for access to that which you would not otherwise have had. There's nothing wrong with this being one of the reasons why you want to play in college. However, if this is your sole reason for wanting to play your sport – meaning that if there were other means to overcome the tuition concerns you would not want to continue playing – then do the following: (a) read the rest of this book, and (b) talk to your school counselor and specific college admissions counselors about financial aid, academic and other scholarships, and work-study programs that can all help reduce the cost of attending college. When student-athletes continue at the college level solely because they need the scholarship money, the transactional nature of the relationship can cause added pressure and stressors that can diminish your college experience.

A few student-athletes will want to continue in college because they see it as a step to play professionally or compete internationally (like in the Olympics). While I can't speak to the paths to a professional career in regards to specific colleges, I would encourage you to have an honest conversation with both your high school (or club) coach and the college coach(es) for whom you are considering playing for. They should be able to give you a clear picture on the prospects to reach these goals, and help you determine your collegiate direction.

Finally, many of the student-athletes that I have worked with have expressed the desire to connect with a team as a reason for wanting to play in college. During high school these athletes have enjoyed the connection and camaraderie shared within their team, and they look forward to forming new friendships in college. This is a powerful reason to continue playing, and this is often sustainable when the student-athlete begins participating at the collegiate level. When camaraderie is as important, or more important, than recognition or playing time, the student-athlete has the opportunity to meet one's goals with or without receiving the playing time that you had during your previous high school season.

There are many reasons why a student-athlete will want to play in college, and my encouragement to you as you determine whether or not collegiate athletics is for you would be to "examine your why." Combine the answers you came up with for these first two questions and think about whether or not that will empower and drive you as you move on to the next level. If your answers are honest, then they aren't "right" or "wrong" at this point in time. Rather, they are simply indicators to help you choose wisely. The following questions will also help in your evaluation, but they are secondary to knowing where you stand on these first two.

What Am I Looking For In A College Outside Of My Sport?

For the college student-athlete, at least for those who are successful in both the classroom and athletically, the two major priorities throughout each year will be (1) academic work, and (2) athletic activity. This goes without saying – in fact, you would not be reading this book if you didn't understand this basic principle. However, what many don't consider in choosing a college is the life outside of simply academic and athletic time. I have had a handful of athletes go to a school only to transfer, not because of grades or even their athletic opportunities, but because they found that they did not like the school very much. Often this was because of location (too far or too close to home, "in the middle of nowhere"), yet sometimes it was due to academic programming ("doesn't offer my major").

So with this question, I would encourage you to list, in writing, some of the key components of what you are looking for in a school. Make three columns. The first column should be must-haves or non-negotiables. These are the things you absolutely want to have in your school. They are so important that if they do not exist, you are likely to cross that school off and no longer consider it an option. If you settle for a school that does not have your non-negotiable components, it is much more likely that you will be unhappy there, no matter how great the athletic opportunity is.

The second column should be titled "Pro's" or "Added Benefits" or something of that nature. This is your list of things that you would like to see at a school, but if they do not exist it will not negate your interest. Things you place here would be amenities and opportunities that will enhance your experience, or possibly give you a career advantage after college. This column should be your longest list. For example, if you want to be a doctor, you might put "close proximity to a hospital or clinic" for easier volunteer or practicum opportunities. This list should include the creature comforts of life – what do you expect in cafeteria food? What can you do on your free time? If you like going to the movies, how important is it for you to be near a movie theater? Do you like the outdoors or the big city? How big of a campus/student body is important to you? How far do you want to have to walk for classes? When you are competing within your sport, how far do you have to travel for away contests? Again, anything and everything that you would like in a college can be listed here. This is a list that you can add to, especially as you visit schools. You might hear of programs or aspects of a school that interest you, and you can add them to this list. This way you can evaluate other schools on whether or not they offer similar things.

The third column is your "Do Not Want" list. This should be a shorter list, similar to the first column. Items you place on this list would prevent you from considering a college if they exist. For some, this starts with geography. If you know of a location that you absolutely do NOT want to be, put that on this list. It will save you plenty of time, money, and stress if you use this to narrow down your choices. This is not your list of things you "don't like" but could live with. How far do you want to be from your family? Does the level of competition matter? Is there an affiliation that you do not want to be associated with? Again, think of this column as "it doesn't matter what the offer or playing time situation is, if _____ exists, then I don't want to go to that school."

Once you've made your list, don't be afraid to alter it as you go on different college visits. While no two schools will be the same, your ultimate decision is going to come down to weighing them against each other, in light of who you are and what you want in a school. A big thing to consider is simply this: when I'm not studying, practicing, training, or competing, what do I see myself doing at this school? Try to envision yourself being there and doing whatever you think you would do on campus. There will be life on campus outside of your academics and your sport, and that time is both needed and valuable to help keep you balanced. Will the school you are considering meet your expectations to allow that free time to be fulfilling?

What Are The Geographical Parameters For College?

This question is as straight forward as it sounds, but I want to break it down a little. Often when I start a recruiting conversation with a student-athlete and his/her family, the feeling is that we are going to go fishing for athletic interest across the entire country. While we can do this, it does not usually generate the results we want, nor is it a good use of our time. As mentioned above, if there is a part of the country where you have no interest in spending your college years, identify this and cross those schools off the list.

This is also where both the student-athlete and the parent, separately, should answer the key question: How far away is acceptable? Don't be afraid to come together and have separate answers, and talk through them. As a coach and a teacher, I tend to lean on the side of having the student-athlete go where he/she chooses, even if it's further than the parent wants. However, I always encourage players and their parents to talk this through, so that even if the decision is not what the other wants, each can understand how the other feels. One note on this – pretty much every college is about 5 hours away at the furthest (at least this is one way that I help parents/players frame distance). If the school is within 300 miles, that's a five hour drive. If its' beyond that, the student is likely flying between home and school, and you can fly pretty much anywhere within the United States in 4 hours or less.

This does also lead us to the question about the importance and ability for your family and friends to attend your athletic events. Like the question above, this will most likely need to be answered separately and then discussed. How often does the school you are considering play within a reasonable driving distance for your family? What is the athletic program's expectation for breaks (summer, spring, Christmas) and your ability to be with or visit your family and friends?

Don't let these questions overwhelm you, as I realize that this question alone can cause either confusion or friction when it comes up for discussion. Remember, your answers to these questions can change. I've seen several student-athletes visit a college that was "too far" in both the athlete's and the parents' eyes, only to fall in love with the campus and for all parties to come to the same conclusion that it was the right school. At the same time, I've seen parents allow their player to explore a college that's seems to be too far, and then the athlete himself comes to the conclusion that it's not a good fit. I'm not advocating for staying close to home or moving far away, but rather I'm highlight the importance of addressing this aspect of a school as part of your decision making process.

What Do I Want To Do After College? Does This Influence My Playing Sports?

It is not uncommon for high school students to have an unclear picture of what they want to major in or what they want to do after college. Especially if you are reading this as a high school freshman or sophomore, don't panic if this question does not have a clear answer yet. If you are of the mindset that you have a few different fields that you are interested in, and that your sports decision will influence which of those paths you choose, that's also perfectly fine. Our world is ever-changing, as are career fields and job opportunities, so it is all right to not be totally set on a singular destination at this point.

With that being said, this question is directed more so to those who have a very strong conviction on what they want to do after college. For some this is graduate school, and for others it is a specific job. If this is you, then you need to consider how your plans for after college may overlap with your sports participation. If there is an overlap, this does not mean that you cannot play your sport, but it does mean that you will need to get some clarification on how to balance this situation.

For example, if you are going into education and you are also a baseball player. In the spring of your senior year, you will likely be given a student-teaching assignment, which may carry a time commitment that overlaps with practices and/or games. Since you know you want to be a teacher, talking to the coach or other players who are in a similar field can help you figure out how to make this potential conflict work. If you plan to work in the medical field and need to accumulate a certain number of practicum hours, you will want to see how others in the same situation have been able to meet both the athletic and academic expectations.

When you have these conversations with coaches or players at a particular college, do not assume that the process is the same at different colleges. There are some situations that are easier to balance than others, and for you not to be surprised a year or two into your college career, you want to get straight answers before making your college decision. Unfortunately, I have seen some student-athletes change their major in college, not because they changed their mind on what they want to do, but because it fit better with their athletic schedule. Then, upon graduating with a degree in a field they don't really enjoy, they find themselves trying to career switch fairly quickly out of college. This often involves additional schooling and additional cost, which could have been avoided had the necessary conversations occurred during the recruiting phase.

What Financial Considerations Are Needed In Selecting A College?

One of the myths that we will cover later involves the misconception that athletic scholarships are always full scholarships. The truth is that a large majority of the opportunities to play a sport in college will come with a financial cost. I've even had FCS football players receive a partial scholarship where they have to figure out how to pay for the remaining tuition, room and board, and academic fees. This is not something to be scared of, but it is something to be aware of as it may guide your decision.

Before I move any further into this section, I want to comment that I always strongly encourage my athletes and their families to consider the cost of attending a school as one of the last factors in the decision making process. Many schools, for whatever reason, have an eye-popping tuition. Do not let this discourage you, and please don't let this be the only reason you would cross a school off your list. Many of the "expensive" schools take pride in the fact that very few of their students pay that listed price. Instead, they pride themselves on the grants and scholarships, along with aid packages, that they grant their students every year. In addition, for many schools, when they offer their initial aid package, if you counter with a request for additional aid, they may be able to add to the amount offered.

For example, I had a student who wanted to attend a school with a total annual cost of $55,000. When she received her aid package, it dropped the tuition to $25,000. This was still more expensive than what her family could afford, so one simple phone call to the school (not sport related) dropped her annual tuition to $12,000. She received a great education and loved her time there. But just think of the opportunity missed had she never applied because of the published cost of attending that school. This is why I encourage you to examine the colleges you are interested in first, and then evaluate what the real cost of attending is going to be (and whether or not this works for you).

Parents: I know the question you have in your head right now – "What if my son or daughter falls in love with a school only to find out that we can't afford it? That will crush his/her dreams." First off, it won't crush their dreams. Second, this is possible but not probable. When you set your financial parameters for school, you will have established what the cost of attendance must come down to, and your child will know going in to a visit that a school is possible only if the cost can get within your pre-established range. When you visit the school, ask about the aids and grants available. Ask how much financial aid the average student receives, and ask what the aid is based on. These conversations will help you have an idea as to whether or not an "expensive" school can drop to within your budget.

One final thought about the cost of attendance: is it a private school or a public school? In my experience, the private schools generally tend to come with a higher cost of tuition, but they also have much greater flexibility in the types and amounts of aids/grants that they can offer students. Often if a college is a public school, most (if not all) of their aid/grant packages are based on standard criteria that is not very flexible. But at the same time, the starting cost for a public school is usually less than competing private schools. All in all, you should always take into consideration your out-of-pocket cost for attending college, but do not be afraid to explore schools that come with some sticker shock because it is unlikely that will be your real cost of attendance.

What Are My Training Habits In Regards To My Sport?

Up to this point, all of the previous questions have centered around your (the athlete and family) perspective and how to think about what you are looking for in a school. The following questions shift to focus on a self-evaluation of how you project as a member of a collegiate athletic program. This question is critically important.

- What type of athletic training do you do?
- How often do you do it?
- Is it a regulated and scheduled workout or training?
- Is it a program that you designed or are you working with a trained professional?

All of these are important. In high school, participation is almost always based on your school's population and the group of students who sign up to participate in your sport. At the college level, teams are made up of individuals who not only choose to play the sport, but athletes who have been chosen (recruited) by the coaching staff to be given that opportunity. To be blunt, the coach does not have to recruit you, and he or she does not have to keep you on their team after choosing their school. This question is directed at the heart of whether or not you have the habits to be successful at the collegiate level.

For most high school athletes, their workout and training regimen is provided by their school, program, or club team. This likely entails a designed program over a set period of time, aimed at reaching specific performance goals. And once this program has concluded, it is scaffolded with another similar training program to continue building on the growth that has occurred.

What has been your history with training? Do you look forward to your workouts? Even if you don't like your workouts, are you consistently attending and putting in the work to improve? I tell my athletes all the time, this is the **base expectation** at the college level. Because the disparity between the top high school athlete and his/her back-up is often quite distinct in high school, athletes can often get away with mediocre training habits and keep their starting spot or role on the high school team. This doesn't fly in college. So it is important to look at what your dedication and effort is, and determine if you are willing and committed to being all in with a training program. If you want your off-season to be a rest without training, then your collegiate athletic activity should be guided to intramurals over intercollegiate competition.

A few years ago, I had two of the top football prospects in the state of Minnesota. When Big 10 coaches would come in, they would often ask to come in during our workouts (we work out before school). The reason for this is that they wanted to see that my athletes were present, and then to observe their work ethic within the workout. One coach arrived to see one of my athletes walk in 5-minutes late to the workout and then the athlete chose to sit out for the running component of the workout. The coach looked at me and said, "Thanks for your time – I've seen all I need to see, so I'm going to head out." I understood what he was seeing. My player was comparable with the top players in the Midwest at his position, but coaches who have one scholarship offer to extend are going to give it to the player that "checks all the boxes" and training habits are one of the big boxes.

You should also understand the college coach's perspective that training habits are a reflection of your other character traits and habits. For many, working out is not the most enjoyable experience, but it is one that demonstrates the ability to do what needs to be done in order to be successful. It's the willingness to pay the price for greatness. To most coaches, the student who is lazy in the classroom will be lazy in workouts and will be volatile at best in practices. This is not attractive. Sure, some coaches take the risk on talented but lazy players, but given the choice of talent that works hard versus talent that sometimes works… the choice is easy. So yes, your high school coach or club coach wants you to be diligent in your in-season and off-season training because it helps prepare you and the team for competition. If you are an athlete with college aspirations, I encourage you to lean into this expectation and make it part of who you are. Again, this will be the base expectation when you are given the opportunity to compete as a college student-athlete.

What if your training has been subpar up to this point? First off, there is a path forward if you are willing to simply acknowledge this fact and commit to changing moving forward. Next, talk to your high school or club coach about appropriate training regimens, and set a training plan that works for your current abilities. Once this is set, follow through and keep records of it. Set your goals and mark growth. When you talk to a potential college coach, have an accurate picture of where you are at and what you are doing in your training, and be able to communicate this.

Note: Most college coaches will prefer to see you train with your team, not on your own. If you have a private training regimen, it should be in addition to your team workouts or in place because you do not have team workouts available (your team doesn't offer them). There are some outstanding private training programs, and I'm not knocking those. Our program contracts our off-season program out to a local company with an outstanding reputation. However, they run the program at our school with our whole team. Some of our athletes will seek supplemental training above and beyond what we do at school at this company's facility. All of this works within what a college coach wants to see. What they do not want to see is an athlete who "knows better," who trains with a family member (no matter how qualified), or who comes across as entitled or believing he/she is better than his/her team which leads to training off-site. Remember, coaches who recruit you are going to be projecting how you will fit in with their team, in-season and out, and a large part of this is your commitment to buy into and participate in their training program. Quite frankly, athletes who do not meet training expectations will not remain on the team at most colleges.

How Would My Teammates And My Coach Describe Me?

In your high school (or club) experience, you have spent countless hours with your coaches and teammates. Who you are has floated to the surface, and they know you better than anyone else, at least within the framework of your sport. It is hard to put up a façade over the course of years, so if a college coach wants to know what you're really like, they will take the opportunity to ask your teammates and coaches about you. If they want to see you in action, they might watch a workout (see above) or come watch you in practices or in a game. And it is sometimes within these situations in which they may take the opportunity to ask about you.

Why do they care about what your teammates think? Well, if your sport is a team sport, the college coach knows that it takes more than talent to put together a successful team. In college, the amount of time you spend with your teammates is significantly greater (and quite possibly under greater pressure) than it was in high school. You will eat, travel, and most likely share a dorm room or an apartment with some of your teammates. The college coach not only wants to see how your athletic ability will mesh within the framework of the other players on the roster, but also how your personality will mesh within the collective personality of the team.

Now, there are a couple of key things to understand here. First, there is no set personality or response that they are looking for, but there are red flags that could cause a college coach a level of concern. You do NOT (and should not) need to pretend to be something that you aren't. There is nothing wrong with being passionate and driven, or demanding that from your teammates (as long as you aren't demanding anything you aren't giving yourself). There's also nothing wrong with being the loud one in the locker room or the reserved one or the nervous one or the celebration dance choreographer. **Be authentic**. The college coach knows the personality of their team, and it's likely you will naturally fit in, whatever that role might be. The red flags come in the form of laziness, not being punctual, and especially one who puts himself/herself (or his/her interests and aspirations) above the team. Even if an athlete's intentions are beneficial (score a lot of points so the colleges notice me), if it comes at the expense of the team, this can be a red flag for the college coach.

Also of note, awards and recognition do not necessarily shed light on who you are to the college coach. For example, if you are "captain" of your team, there are many reasons why you might serve in that role. You might be the most popular or have the most friends on the team, and they have voted you in. You might be the coach's favorite player, and you were designated as a captain because the coach likes you. Or perhaps you're the top (or one of the best) player on your team, so your skill has earned the respect to make you a captain. But does this make you a coachable player or a good teammate? Maybe, but also maybe not. What's the point? I think that many high school athletes wrongly assume that some level of award or recognition verifies the ability and worthiness of a college's attention. Whereas this can certainly help when the coach sees your award or recognition as an outcome of being a coachable player and a great teammate, but it will not stand alone in their evaluation of you.

This question is one for consideration. If you are a younger student-athlete, be intentional about how you allow yourself to be coached, corrected, and encouraged, and be intentional about how you interact with and treat your teammates. This goes a long way. If you are a senior athlete whose season has ended, there's not a lot you can do that will change how those who have played with or coached you experienced you as a member of the team. But it is powerful to understand that moving to the collegiate level will give you another opportunity to be part of a team, and you will either continue or adjust your behaviors and interactions to be a productive and engaged member of that team.

What Are My Participation Expectations In My First Year On Campus?

Before you start looking into potential colleges, I strongly advise you to consider your perspective on what you expect in terms of participation when you get to campus. What do you want your role to be, and how much playing time do you expect to earn or receive? What is your perspective on being a role player, a bench player, or a scout team player that receives limited to no playing time? If the colleges you consider offer a "JV" or local intercollegiate competition option, is that a team you are willing to play on?

College athletics, no matter what level you get the opportunity to play at, is stepping onto a different stage from your high school or club level. In the late 1990's, a small college in Minneapolis had a future NBA draft pick playing on their team. For him, you might assume that for an NBA talent playing Division III basketball, that it would not be a step up for him. You would be incorrect. The teams he played against were bigger, faster, and more physical – let alone more skilled in playing basketball – than the high school teams he played against the year before. While he was, without question, the best basketball player on the court every time they played a game, the competition was still a step up.

As you step up into college athletics, your perspective may need to revert back to a similar perspective to what you had entering high school. Very few freshman that enter our program expect to play varsity football as a 9th grader. However, you would be surprised at how many high school players expect to step on campus and be a standout athlete as a freshman in college. The parallels aren't exact, but they are valid. The incoming 9th grader may have been a standout 8th grader, but he or she usually does not assume to possess varsity level ability upon arrival. The freshman in college is often coming off of a successful high school career, in which he or she feels established as an athlete. Often they do not consider that they are competing for playing time and various roles on the team against 21 to 23 year old adults who have been invested in the team for years. This can lead to frustration and disappointment.

This section is not implying that college freshman do not have the ability or will not get the opportunity to play upon arriving at a college. You could very well play a significant role as soon as you step on campus. It is a fair question to ask your potential college coach what he/she expects for you if you join their program. The answers can vary during recruiting – some coaches will be honest and some will tell you what you want to hear. But if it is something that is a big deal to you, then I strongly urge you to be honest about your questions and concerns when you talk to college coaches. When I have seen great high school athletes become unhappy when they get to college, it is often based in unrealistic expectations or false understandings regarding their playing time or role on the team. Many times this leads to transfers, which all too often are not to a better situation.

The converse is also true. Some of the student-athletes I have seen who have had the greatest experiences at the college level have gone into their freshman year with the right attitude and a proper understanding of how they fit into the team. This has ranged from players who have spent the first two years on the scout team to others who have been immediately inserted into the starting line-up. Playing time, while desired, was not the sole factor in their happiness with their college choice. Instead, because they had conversations with their future college coaches and other teammates (during recruiting visits), they had a clearer understanding of the situation and opportunities that they were joining.

Final Thoughts

Recruiting is a chaotic process – I will intentionally point this out many times throughout this book. When you run into something that does not make sense, it should not come as a surprise. We cannot fully control the recruiting process, but as a coach I often say, "we have to control what we can control." Taking an accurate self-inventory is something that you can control. Knowing who you are, what you want, and where you stand are tools in your recruiting toolbox.

Everyone loves positive attention, especially when it comes to college coaches wanting you to come play for their program. This is a statement on your ability, achievement, and potential. However, I strongly urge you to keep an open mind to possible opportunities, while being clear about schools/programs that do not fit who you are or what you're looking for. Every extra minute you spend engaging with a college that is a poor fit is wasted time at best, and at worst it will only add to the chaotic and confusing component of recruiting. At the same time, when you focus on schools that align with who you are and what you are looking for, this gives you additional time to evaluate them and to explore what it will be like joining that campus and team.

If there are questions that you don't know the answer to, that's fine at this point. Especially if you are a younger student-athlete reading this book. But come back to these and be honest with yourself. This can be enlightening and empowering in the recruiting process. As a coach, my goal and hope is to connect my student-athletes with a great fit for them if they want to play at the college level. The great fit is what will empower them with the future they desire beyond college. My hope is the same for you.

2 LEVELS OF PLAY

This chapter will explore the different levels of play for collegiate sports, as well as briefly touching on governing bodies for collegiate athletics. In looking at levels of play, you will understand the differences between the levels of play in a way that is practical and useful.

Governing Bodies

The most prominent governing body for collegiate athletics is the National Collegiate Athletic Association or the **NCAA**. From my experience, and for the purposes of this book, this is the governing body that I will spend the most time referencing. The NCAA website is **ncaa.org** and there is a great amount of detail about their organization on their website. I am not going to regurgitate information that can be found online, but rather my aim in this chapter is to help prospective college student-athletes and their parents understand the differences in levels of play.

Within the NCAA there are three divisions for competition: Division I, Division II, and Division III. Within each division are conferences, or groups of schools that regularly compete with each other. In addition to intercollegiate competition, many schools may also offer **club** and/or **intramural** opportunities. Club competition is not officially sponsored by a school, but involves members of the student-body (many times covering their own expenses for competition). Intramural opportunities are similar to a community "in-house" program where students form their own teams and compete in more leisurely competition. For the purpose of this book, we will not be covering Club or Intramural opportunities. Should you want to stay involved in your sport with significantly less pressure and expectations, then consult with your college about these opportunities.

In addition to the NCAA, two other governing bodies are the National Junior College Athletic Association or **NJCAA** and the National Association of Intercollegiate Athletics or the **NAIA**. There are two main reasons why a student-athlete would choose to attend a Junior College to continue his or her career: (1) they need to improve academically to become eligible or viable for a school at the level they desire, and/or (2) they want another opportunity to be evaluated and recruited by traditional four-year schools. While I will outline eligibility requirements and issues in a later chapter, one should be aware that collegiate (NCAA) eligibility is used up during seasons played under other governing bodies. So a player who plays for a Junior College for two years, has two years of eligibility remaining to play at a different school.

In an effort to be transparent, I have never recommended nor had a player choose to attend an NAIA school for football. I have had NAIA coaches contact me and compare their level of play to NCAA Division II, but that is primarily because they are able to offer scholarships and have different – seemingly more relaxed – requirements for eligibility. In terms of ability to compete, I believe that NAIA is closer to the lower part of Division III NCAA schools. There are schools in my state that were previously NAIA who switched to NCAA, and compete in the lower echelon of the Division III schools in our area. In addition, many of the NAIA scholarships that I have seen issued offer a large dollar amount, only to find out that the starting price is significant. For example, I had a football player get an NAIA offer in writing for a $30,000 scholarship, only to find out that the cost of attendance was around $65,000. Both the player and I questioned if it was really a valuable scholarship or not. I am sure that the quality of education is fine at NAIA schools, and there are certainly reasons for schools to choose to not be in the NCAA. Just in my experience, when high school student-athletes are having questions about the recruiting process and want to play at the next level, they are almost exclusively talking about playing at an NCAA institution.

NCAA Division I

In general, Division I schools are larger colleges and universities that can support multiple programs. At the time of this writing, there are 347 Division I colleges and universities, but not every Division I school offers every sport. These can be larger research universities or smaller, wealthier schools who can afford to provide the scholarships and technical funding to support multiple programs. This funding may come from strong alumni networks, endowments, or access to television contracts. When you turn on Saturday afternoon football games, Wednesday night basketball double headers, or the NCAA Baseball or Softball World Series – these are Division I schools. In terms of competition, Division I competition usually features the highest talent level, performs in front of the largest crowds, and is more easily recognizable on the national stage. When a Division I school recruits a student-athlete, they believe that he or she can help their team compete at the highest level.

For Division I schools, student-athletes can be offered both scholarships and walk-on opportunities. Division I sports have a roster size limit, and sports are allowed to offer a certain number of scholarships. While football has a different Division I breakdown, scholarships offered by Division I schools are full-scholarships. This means that the scholarship will include tuition, fees, and room and board. Some conferences and schools have expanded their rules to also cover the "true cost of attendance" and provide a stipend to student-athletes to cover what the school determines to be the reasonable cost for their athletes to travel home and cover basic expenses. This does not have to be offered by a school offering a scholarship. If a Division I school offers a player a walk-on, or more prominently known as a PWO (Preferred Walk On) it means that the coach is saving a roster spot for this player. We will talk about this option later in this book.

In football only, Division I is broken into two divisions: **Football Bowl Subdivision** (formerly Division I-A) and the **Football Championship Subdivision** (formerly Division I-AA). The FBS is the level of Division I football that ends its season with a Bowl Game for approximately half of its membership. FBS teams have to qualify by winning six games – "becoming bowl eligible" – and then they will get to choose to accept or decline an invitation to a Bowl Game as their last game of the season. This level of football is the highest level of college football, and these teams are what you see on your television on Saturdays. Another important understanding of FBS football is that each team is allowed 85 scholarships, and these must be "full" scholarships. This allows for 20 additional roster spots to be non-scholarship or walk-on student-athletes.

The FCS level of play is the subdivision of Division I football that ends its season with a tournament style playoff system to determine a national champion. If a school is an FCS school, they are allotted up to 63 scholarships to issue to their football players. Whereas the FBS level requires all scholarships to be "full" this is not the case at the FCS level. Coaches can break up scholarships to offer partial scholarships (i.e. 1 scholarship = 2 players each getting 50%). In addition, FCS schools do not have to offer scholarships. There are leagues and independent schools that compete in the FCS that do not offer scholarships. One non-scholarship league is the well-known Ivy League (Harvard, Yale, Princeton, etc).

If you are exploring an FCS school for football, do a little research to determine whether or not the school can offer you an athletic scholarship. One tactic I have seen employed by FCS schools is the combination of a "cost of attendance allowance" combined with a partial scholarship (say 70%) which will come out to covering the full cost of tuition, room & board, and fees. This gives FCS schools more scholarships to offer that will feel like they are full scholarships, but the assumption is that the player will use the COA stipend to cover the remaining costs of school, and not living costs like travel home, groceries, or other daily needs.

Division II

The major difference between Division I and Division II schools is most widely seen in the funding afforded athletic programs. At the time of this writing, there are 312 Division II schools. These schools can still offer athletic scholarships, but will be more limited in their availability. Often Division II schools will offer partial scholarships, and then they will seek to add other types of aid (grants, merit-based scholarships, etc.) on top to attract student-athletes. While pretty much every sport offered by a Division I school can be offered by a Division II school, you will need to check to make sure that the Division II school you are interested in offers your sport. In all likelihood, if you are reading this book and have a Division II school that you're interested in, you already know that they offer your sport.

As mentioned above, the big difference is funding. We see this in the number of scholarships allotted for Division II schools. For example, in football, Division II schools are allowed by the NCAA to offer up to 32 scholarships; however, many Division II schools are allotted less by their administration (for example, they might only be given 16 scholarships to break up to give to their players). There are many reasons for this including overall enrollment, fees collected from students and organizations, Title IX legislation requirements, and revenue generated from a given sport or the athletic department as a whole.

In addition to a difference in the type and amount of scholarships, you will likely notice a difference in the size (and perhaps quality) of the facilities of Division II schools compared to Division I schools. Stadiums and arenas will likely be smaller, due in large part to the average attendance for athletic events. Locker rooms, weight rooms, and training facilities may be more limited at Division II schools, which is also a reflection of funding.

There can be some benefits of Division II schools (depending upon what you are looking for) that include a smaller overall student-body, which can mean smaller class sizes. Many public Division II schools have lower tuition cost than their (even same school system) Division I comparisons. And the travel distance for most Division II athletic conferences is significantly shorter than that of larger Division I conferences. This means less time on the road for competitions, and for many student-athletes allows family and friends greater access to watch them compete on a regular basis.

Division III

Division III schools do not offer athletic scholarships, and many of them are private schools. Division III schools offer a wide variety of sports, and there is a wide disparity of funding between different Division III schools. Some schools will be well funded and offer a number of highly competitive teams, and others are poorly funded and programs are consistently in jeopardy of being reduced or cut from one year to the next. The scholarships that Division III can issue are not specifically tied to athletic involvement or performance. This means that the aid can be need-based, merit-based, or earned through being granted other scholarship means that are open to the whole student body (or prospective students) to apply for.

For the student-athlete wanting to continue to play your sport in college, the idea of a school not having athletic scholarships may be a negative. However, I would encourage you to consider a different perspective. It is highly likely that you will qualify for grants, aid, or scholarships based on your grades, test scores, and/or other merit-based worthiness (i.e. Leadership Scholarship). This scholarship amount will often exceed the athletic amount that a Division II school can offer you. The difference here is that your academic performance (usually GPA) will keep the aid at the Division III school, where the athletic aid can be increased or decreased every year at a Division I or Division II school. In essence, you control keeping your aid at the Division III level. Also, as your life changes, if you choose to no longer play your sport at your college, the Division III aid would still be in place (whereas you would lose your athletic scholarship at a Division I or II school if you chose to stop playing).

As stated above, the quality of the athletic programs vary from school to school, so I would strongly encourage you to get on campus and see the differences for yourself. For my Division I and Division II athletes, I also encourage them to investigate one or two high level Division III schools to be able to compare. For the Division III schools that receive excellent funding for their athletic programs, their facilities are often comparable to Division I facilities. In 2007 I had a player who had an FCS offer to play football, and I encouraged him to visit Mount Union which is a Division III powerhouse. He returned from the visit and adamantly stated that the facilities at Mount Union were far superior to the FCS school he was looking at. He still took the FCS scholarship opportunity, but had that not worked out as he wished, he would have been excited to play at a Division III school.

If you have a Division III school or schools that you are interested in, I always encourage my student-athletes to apply as soon as you have interest, and then request your financial aid package. Because many of the Division III schools are private schools, they may carry a higher listed tuition price. This price will not be your cost to attend (most likely). Get to the bottom line and then compare the cost of schools. I'm a big believer in getting the facts in front of you so that you can make the choice that meets your needs and desires.

Final Thoughts

There are literally hundreds of options of schools that have your sport and may be able to provide the opportunity to play your sport in college. However, try to narrow your focus as soon as you can. Your coaches, and the attention you start to receive from college coaches, will help you know which division is an accurate one for your ability. Don't worry about Division. In today's world, being able to promote things you think are prestigious – like the kids who tweet out every "offer" they receive – can take your focus off what will make you happy. **Your goal in the recruiting process should be to find a school that is a great academic, athletic, and social fit for you, and to be excited about your future at that school.** Everything else is just noise. A lot will go into your college decision, but try to ignore the pressure to "play at the highest level" if there is a better fit for you somewhere else.

Parents, I strongly urge you to be on board with that statement above, too. If your child has the ability and desire to play Division I sports – that's awesome and enjoy the ride. However, if they are more suited for Division II or Division III opportunities, don't allow them to miss those opportunities because your ego wants them to focus on Division I. Whatever level they choose to play at is not a referendum on your athletic or parenting ability. The joy of watching your child compete that got them into the sport years ago should be the motivation that you bring to the recruiting process. Helping your child find the right fit will be so much more rewarding than anything else in this process. For many, if they don't feel the need to try to make you proud with a level of play, but rather they feel your love, pride, and support from them simply continuing, they are empowered and lean in to an incredible college experience at whichever level they fit.

3 BEING A COLLEGE ATHLETE

So far we've covered a Self-Inventory in Chapter 1, and we've looked at different levels of play within the NCAA in Chapter 2. This chapter is meant to serve as a "reality check" before we move into more detailed information on the recruiting process. If the life outlined below is not what you are looking for in your college life, then I encourage you to have more detailed conversations with your coach(es) and family members. Many like the recruiting process because it provides wanted, often deserved, positive attention for all of the work you have put into playing your sport. But it is simply a **transitional process** by which you are determining your next level of play.

This chapter will not cover the physical ability of your teammates and your opponents, but when considering some of the information outlined, it is important to understand why the college athletic life looks like this. You are now competing against young adults, and not teenagers. To be successful at this level requires an increased focus, work ethic, and dedication. For example, in-season my high school football players have roughly 14 hours per week of football: 3 hours of lifting, 2 hours of film, 6 hours of practice, and one game that lasts approximately 3 hours. We ask our kids to independently watch 2 additional hours of film over the course of 6 days. So for an "all in" varsity football player, their time commitment is 16 hours per week. In college, in-season athletes should expect 20 hours of "required" activity from their sport, and this does not include other time commitments that are inherently related to your sport.

Time Management is the most important skill that any prospective college student should have upon arriving on campus, and it is only magnified for those who participate in sports. Part of my teaching assignment is a concurrent enrollment course with the University of Minnesota. The University's syllabus explicitly states that for every credit taken, a student should expect 2 hours per week of study outside of the course to be successful. To put this in perspective, to be a full-time student (which is required for athletic participation) you will be taking a minimum of 12 semester credits. This means that the university thinks that you will have an additional 24 hours of studying. Many students will take 16 semester credits which is an additional 32 hours of studying every week.

Now, before this gets overwhelming, remember that in college you won't spend seven hours per day sitting in a desk. Your classes will likely meet two or three times per week, and you will usually get to choose the time of your class when you choose your schedule. So your high school week saw 35 hours in class, but you will likely be in class about 12 to 15 hours per week in college. The extra time for studying is built into your day. But will YOU build it into your day to stay on top of your studies? Can you plan your schedule to allow for your academic, athletic, and social requirements? As the ancient proverb states, if you "fail to plan, you are planning to fail."

Many times an athletic program will help you set up your schedule – both in choosing your classes and in helping establish a plan for your academic load. Most athletic programs will connect you with an academic counselor – sometimes employed by either the athletic department or your specific sports team within the university – to help navigate your dual expectations. They will help you choose classes that don't conflict with practice or training times, and they can equip you with the tools (writing lab, tutors, etc) that can help equip you for success. For example, many programs will have mandatory study hall (aka study table) times that athletes are required to attend. This is the intentional building in of time set aside for academic work.

Even with available help, it will be up to you to seek out additional help and to organize your unregulated time to allow you to meet your requirements. For example, you will need to plan your travel time to and from your classes, your residence (dorm, apartment, home, etc), and your athletic facilities. In high school, it's likely that you were a two-minute walk from anywhere you need to be. In college, you might have classes blocks apart in different buildings, followed by a practice on the other side of campus. You'll need to plan your day accordingly.

In addition, time outside of the required obligations is difficult to manage if you don't have a plan to get into a routine. I strongly recommend that you plan a time for study that meets your personality and current habits. For example, if you are a morning person, I recommend scheduling earlier classes where you can get some studying done after class and before practice. If you need to sleep in and are a night owl, you can set your plan around that. There is a lot more freedom in college, but this freedom can set you up for failure if it ends up as wasted time.

When it comes to the off-season, you will be **expected to be a full-time participant in the off-season training program**. This will include strength and speed training, along with sport-specific training sessions (possibly with or without the coaches present). Therefore, time management is critical throughout your year, not just while your sport is in-season. As mentioned before, full participation in the off-season training program is a base expectation, and serious college athletes have full buy in to this expectation. The overall time required in the off-season will be more limited than in-season requirements, but it will still be a significant weekly time commitment.

Another consideration is the **social scene**. Our pop culture has led most young people to see college as a roller coaster between academic work in the day to a weekly four-day, often alcohol infused party on the weekend. While this can be your experience, do not expect to experience a significant amount of academic or athletic success if this is your routine. But don't worry, this is not an "either-or" choice. When selecting a school, think about and ask current students what they do with their free time. Talk to athletes in the program you would join what they do with free time. This can give you an accurate picture of what your options are. As a student-athlete on campus, you will have more limited options when 20-30 hours of what would be free-time for others is committed to your sport. One final thought is to look at the geographic and general characteristics of the school and to think about your free-time. The small, Christian college located in a rural area will have a different free time social life than the large liberal arts school located in the heart of a big city. The types of free time activities available, and your interest in them, will help you determine how much free time will be spent on social activities versus other non-athletic activities such as working or studying.

Finally, as a prospective college athlete, you should also understand the varying nature of your future coaches. The recruiting process may or may not give you an accurate picture of what your coach will be like when you are on the team. Some coaches will take an "ends justifies the means" approach in recruiting and tell you whatever you want to hear to get you to choose their school. This happens more than you think. I don't include that to create pessimism when talking to coaches, but a healthy level of skepticism is appropriate. When you get the opportunity to visit a school, ask to have a chance to talk to a current member of the team. Often this will be part of a recruiting visit, and to me, it would be a red flag if this wasn't offered by a school when you visit campus. Within the past few years, that athlete was in your very shoes in trying to choose a school, ended up choosing the school you are visiting, and will be honest in telling you the positive and negative aspects of that decision. I think this is very valuable and can help you see what life is really like on campus. Ask about free time, social life, practice expectations, course load, schedule planning, academic support tools (even if you think you don't need or want them), and coaching style.

Please don't misunderstand what I'm saying here... there are plenty of "what you see is what you get" coaches at the college level, so you may have the straight forward recruiting process. In all likelihood, you will experience both types of coaches during the recruiting process and it is difficult to tell which is which. Too often student-athletes and parents will choose to favor the opportunity by the coach who makes everything sound great, when in reality this might not be the best situation. Again, evaluate everything that you are interested in, just know that the relationship with the coach does change – for better or worse – when your relationship has gone from pursuit to player.

I bring this distinction up in this chapter on what it's like to be a college athlete because I think all college student-athletes should go into this experience with his/her eyes open. In high school, whether you had a positive relationship with your high school coach or not, coaching was not their sole occupation. This doesn't mean that they put in less time or effort, but rather that the employment that pays their bills and puts food on their table was not in jeopardy if the team had a down year. At the college level, it is extremely likely that your coach's sole occupation is coaching your college team. Recruiting the right athletes for their program is literally job security. If you are playing at a school on an athletic scholarship, there is a transactional relationship between you and the coach's program: they help pay for your school and you help them win athletic contests.

Because you spend significantly more time involved with your sport at the college level, it is quite possible that you will become very close with your college coach. However, it is also possible that you may never feel the same connection you felt in high school due to the transactional nature of collegiate sports. Your college coach, to keep his or her job, needs to recruit someone who they think is better than you, at your position, every year. This does not mean that they don't like you or that they don't truly hope for you to be successful. But high performing programs are always using competition to make their program better. **Expect this**. Don't be afraid of competition, and realize that you are being recruited to come in and compete with players already on the roster, and the same thing will happen once you are a player on the roster. While I think this reality makes sense to most high school student-athletes, I want you to enter your situation aware that it might "feel" different depending upon your personality, your coach's personality, and the culture of your team.

Final Thoughts

All in all, playing your sport in college can be an incredible opportunity and experience. You can make friendships that will last a lifetime, and you can continue to grow as a person and as an athlete. To be successful you will have to have a plan, and develop a routine, that will empower your habits to drive your behavior. This does not happen by accident, and you should work on this right away. I would even argue that you could start to do this to some extent before you leave high school. In addition, be prepared to spend greater time, with greater intensity, on your sport. This is where your answer to the first two questions in Chapter 1 come into play. And finally, be prepared to build a different relationship with your coach. This might be stronger or more distant than what you have previously experienced, but just know that it will be different. The nature of the job requires it to be. But this does not mean that it will be worse, nor that it will be detrimental to your development. Just expect to build a new relationship with your coach (as you will with your new teammates) that will take time and need to persevere through adversity to grow stronger.

4 RECRUITING MYTHS & MISUNDERSTANDINGS

As I stated at the beginning of this book, the recruiting process will be chaotic and can be confusing. One of the major culprits of the confusion centers around **myths and misunderstandings**. For many student-athletes, their understanding of the recruiting process is what they see on social media or whatever half-truths have been marketed to them through recruiting services. When I give my presentations on recruiting to student-athletes at my school, I highlight this information as much or more than anything else.

No matter how much noise these make, or how attractive they sound, you will find much greater peace and direction in the recruiting process when you **disregard the myths and grasp the real understandings**. You may need to come back to this chapter in the future.

Unfortunately, some of the places that you would naturally turn are not helpful when it comes to some of these topics. Many of the school counselors that I have worked with have a limited understanding of collegiate eligibility, at best. The same can be said for some coaches. In fact, one of the best coaches I've ever known starts each year's parent meeting by telling his families that, "it's not my job to get your kid a chance to play in college." I understand his sentiment, but in my own coaching I strongly disagree. His point is that his focus needs to be on his team and his program as a holistic and special experience, not a transitional experience for future college athletes. He has had some great high school players become great college players, but his assistance to them along the path of the recruiting process is very limited. When these common outlets for guidance become limited or unavailable, then student-athletes and families often open themselves up to outside services or myths, almost all of which will do more harm than good.

Put it this way: I feel so strongly about this that if there is a question about the veracity of something that I don't cover in this book, email me and I will let you know how it stacks up. I will not offer you a service to buy, and I cannot become your personal recruiting advisor (unless you're one of my players), but I will take the time to give you an honest, truthful response to your question. My email is: **CoachAndrewHill@gmail.com**. If I don't cover it here, but it seems fishy or out of place, shoot me an email and I will be happy to respond.

Myth #1: I am a Diamond in the Rough, and a Recruiting Service will make sure I get noticed.

I am going to devote the entire next chapter to paid recruiting services. You should also note that many who offer a "free profile" also will have higher levels of subscription which promise greater services, that come at a fee. Again, I will address this in the next chapter, but the basic rule of thumb is simple: **avoid recruiting services like you'd avoid the plague.**

This myth is a very powerful one, and quite frankly a myth that many student-athletes want to believe if they are not receiving the recruiting attention they want (or not from the schools they desire). It is also powerful because in the previous generation, there's a good chance for this to be true. However, with the increased access to players through various technological outlets, what was true for my generation and those before me is NOT the truth for today's student-athletes. The second part of this myth – needing a recruiting service to get one's name in the hands of the colleges – strongly exists because of one's willingness to believe that he or she has been overlooked. Even if this offends you, I want you to know that this is NOT the case.

First, every student-athlete should evaluate the highest level at which he or she has played on their high school or club team. If you are not a varsity student-athlete (yet), then you are not a college recruit yet. On your club team, if you are not competing at the highest level, then you are probably not getting exposed to the college coaches who are watching, evaluating, and recruiting from teams who play at that highest level. In my football program, I do not promote a prospective student-athlete until they have **varsity game film** that can be shared that will support my recommendation. This is the standard across the country.

Parents, when I first became a head coach in 2005, my first year was still in the "VHS age" where copying tapes and sending them out to a dozen schools was an expensive, long process. From 2006-2010 was what I call the "DVD age" where I could copy a handful of DVD's in minutes, thus speeding up the process and expanding who and how many prospect films I could send out for an athlete. Then, around 2010 the "Digital Video Age" has started and there's no end in sight. Programs now store and edit game film on platforms like *HUDL* and can share this out with a couple of clicks. When I send out my annual prospect report, it contains Hudl highlight links for each individual athlete, and it goes to over 250 schools in a 12-state region. Coaches can also search for my athletes on Hudl or Google and have their highlights pop up. If your child has the film to back up their ability, college coaches can (and usually will) watch it. Creating an attractive highlight film is extremely important (see Chapter 9).

This is the point where, at least when I get contacted by student-athletes at rival schools, the statement gets made that "my coach isn't doing anything to help get my name out there." Well, I cannot speak for or against other coaches and what they do, but I can tell you that your coach is not the only voice that helps college coaches pay attention to you as a prospective student-athlete. When a college coach visits me, we will spend a good chunk of time talking about the other athletes in the area that I know about or have heard about. I include this in my interaction because I believe that gives my recommendations credibility, and it keeps college coaches coming to my building whether or not I have kids they are interested in. My point is this – if you are a "can't miss" prospect, other coaches will bring up your name as well.

In addition, if there are schools that you are interested in, you can look up their coaching staff and see which coach is your position coach and which coach recruits the area in which you live. Reach out to those coaches, introduce yourself, include a **varsity highlight film** link, and tell them that you would love to explore their school as a prospective student-athlete. Now, I STRONGLY recommend that you talk to your coach before doing this, if for nothing other than to give him or her a heads up. This will help you get noticed, and coaches will likely give you an initial evaluation. It does not mean they will "offer" you or continue to recruit you, but they might. If they like what they see, they will reach out to your coach to get some more information on your academic and athletic performance. Again, I strongly encourage you to work with your high school coach in this part of the process, but know that you are not isolated in ways to make this introduction.

Now, on behalf of myself and all of the other coaches out there, I have to let you know that plenty of players, and more often it is the parents, are delusional about their ability and what would be a good fit at the college level. I see way too many players in different sports at different schools pass up great Division II or Division III opportunities because they are holding out for the Division I opportunity. Granted, there are players who should wait and do this, but many others have never heard from a Division I school and are foolishly holding out hope. As a coach, I will be optimistically honest with my players. We will shoot for the highest, realistic level of play. Most of my parents and players that go through this process are onboard, but some will continue to visit Big 10 schools when their player would make a great Northern Sun Conference (Division II) player. So please, start this process with a conversation with your coach. And note that if you are a Division I player, but for some reason your coach doesn't think so, that other coaches will speak to your ability. In the meantime, talk with your own coach about what needs to change in your own abilities or behaviors to be considered a Division I prospect.

Finally, to address the second half of this myth – that recruiting services can bridge the gap for you – this is just not true. Will recruiting services take your money, make you a webpage with your contact information and possibly highlight film, yes. Do colleges look at this? I can tell you that in my 15 years of being a head high school coach, that I have NEVER had a college reach out to me because they were referred to one of my student-athletes through a recruiting service. Long story short, they promise a lot and deliver little, only to turn around and blame the high school program or coach for not delivering. Any recruiting work that gets done will come back to your high school (or possibly club) coach for a recommendation. So why pay for a service to get you right back to where I'm telling you the starting point is?

Myth #2: There are so many scholarships out there, I just have to find mine.

This is another myth perpetuated by both online hype and recruiting services. The word "offer" implies a full scholarship offer, when in reality, if it is true, simply means that a head coach of a program has offered to save a spot on his or her team for the student-athlete. It does not mean a scholarship offer, and it is not unlimited in terms of time or spots. Many schools will "offer" dozens of capable players for a single spot, only to fill it with the first who "commits." But beware, if this commitment is simply verbal and a different prospect who the college evaluates as a better player wants that spot, offers tend to disappear, sometimes at the last moment. So ignore the social media hype about schools and offers. Work within your own quest and interaction, and don't try to compare your experience to the half-truth that someone else puts out on social media.

Recruiting services, as mentioned above and will later, perpetuate this myth as a reason for needing their services. They do not have access to a secret pile of scholarship money, and they don't have a backdoor into a coach's prospect list upon which they can move your name to the top. A concentrated 30-minute session of Google searches for schools with your sport and preferred program of study will yield more productive results than an onslaught of garbage manufactured from a recruiting service.

There are many colleges which offer your sport at different levels of competition. Some of these schools may offer scholarships, but make no mistake, this is not a game of scholarship musical chairs. Each of these schools that field a team in your sport will fill out its roster, allocate all of the scholarship money they have available, and have members of the team who are participating that are not receiving an athletic scholarship. If you want to earn an athletic scholarship, then you need to have demonstrated the ability to be able to help a team win at the Division I or Division II level; and, the coach of that team needs to choose you over others who are of a similar ability.

Now, if you are not of the mindset that you have to have a scholarship, but simply want to have the options of playing your sport, then you can consider the "walk-on" option of joining the team and not being on scholarship. At the Division III level, every student-athlete is not receiving an athletic scholarship. For others, the desire to play at a certain level might draw them to walk-on and prove that they are worthy of receiving a scholarship. The recruiting process is similar, and there are limited walk-on spots on each team. If you want to consider a walk-on, you need to make sure that you have been somewhat recruited by the school. In order to have a spot on the team – filling one of the few non-scholarship roster spots – you would want to accept an offer to be a "Preferred Walk On" or PWO. To simply walk-on means that you are not guaranteed a spot, many times need to wait for the school year or season to start, and would be part of a tryout process that might not lend any additional spots on the team to those who try out. Parents, as a reference think of the movie *RUDY* (1993) – he was a regular walk on. His story became a movie because of how rare his experience was.

So, to wrap this myth up, to be a scholarship athlete takes a lot of work and requires you to earn it. If you are not offered a scholarship (of any amount) out of high school, but you are offered a PWO spot on the team, then you can continue to try to earn a scholarship as a member or the team. If you simply want to continue your sport in college, that is likely a possibility if you are willing to do your research and connect with the programs that can offer you that opportunity. Simple participation numbers in high school to those of college tell us that spots are limited, so be prepared to communicate with colleges and to perform in front of them to be offered the opportunity to play.

As an example, for my football players I break down this numbers example. If there are 130 FBS football programs that will offer 20 scholarships per year, that would be 2,600 FBS scholarships given each year. If we divide that equally between 50 states (which is not realistic when you compare the prospects from AK to CA) that would be 52 scholarships per state. In Minnesota (my state) alone we name 50 All-State players and over 200 All-State honorable mention players. We have 90 players participate in our All-Star game. So this means that you can be an All-State football player, play in the All-Star game, and simply by numbers not be an FBS Scholarship football player. I don't do this to discourage anybody, I just like to make sure everyone has the right perspective. Maybe the parent of a player planning a college tour might adjust from touring Wisconsin, Northwestern, Nebraska, and Iowa State to that of looking at South Dakota, North Dakota, the University of Minnesota Duluth, and the University of St. Thomas. This is no indictment of talented players, but rather helping people use their time and resources wisely.

Myth #3: I'm better than that player, and they got an offer, so I should get one, too.

This is one of the most confusing parts of the recruiting process. Let this following, counter-intuitive statement sink in:

The best player is not necessarily the best recruit.

This is hard for me to support, but I have found that within the recruiting process this has played out more than you might realize. In 2006 I had a player who was recognized by a media outlet in Virginia as the Virginia State Player of the Year (for Class AA). He did not have any FBS or FCS scholarship offers. While the reasons varied by school, it usually came down to size, and the fact that my player was "maxed out" because he was in great shape, strong, fast, and a good student. These were all the things I loved about him as a coach, and I wouldn't change it. It was frustrating.

Each college program is different, and each coach has different things that he/she is looking for to help make their program better. This means that the recruiting landscape is going to look different from different perspectives.

In my experience, some of the most powerful things that college coaches evaluate is the physical ability for a player to compete successfully at their level, whether or not they demonstrate that skill at a high level in high school. I had a college coach come to a basketball game while recruiting a different player. After watching one of our junior basketball players run, jump, and move quickly – and had the measurables of being tall (6'2") with long arms and big hands – this college coach looked at me and said "You tell him that if he even comes out for football as a senior, I've got a scholarship for him to play receiver for us." This was an FBS coach. This basketball player had never played football (and he never did play) in high school. But the coach saw the potential in his physical ability. Had he come out for football, he would have been a good receiver. But in our conference alone there would be four or five better than him, but he'd be the only one getting an FBS offer. This is some of the chaos involved in recruiting.

 Here's one way to think about it – recruiting is the life blood of the college coach's job security, only second to actually winning games. Even some of the best people in college sports can find themselves out of a job if their work doesn't translate to success. Great teams are made up of great athletes that work together. Most college coaches think they can get the latter to occur, but they need to recruit the great athletes. The common sense principle is that the teams that start off with the best athletes will have more success than the teams that start off with the second tier athletes. You believe this too which is why you cheer for Butler in the Final Four in 2010 and 2011, or why Boise State beating Oklahoma State in the 2007 Fiesta Bowl is so exciting. I would assert that nobody on Butler's roster was offered a scholarship (if they were even looked at) by Duke, yet there they were playing at the highest level. It's exciting because in our minds we don't think that this "should" happen. Why not? Because Duke basketball has access to bring in better players than Butler does. It's that simple. So if we recognize it and believe it to be true, we can't fault college coaches who operate from the same standpoint.

 This is easier said than done. For my state's recruiting class right now, two of the top players in our state are headed to the same FCS school (North Dakota State), while lesser athletes are going to be playing at FBS schools and in the Big 10. I cannot explain this, other than to say that each college coaching staff must have evaluated the potential over the performance of who they chose to offer and not offer. This frustrates me, yet I see it happen every year. But I would also say this – I'm not shocked that the Big 10 school's won't play

North Dakota State any more, and I'm also not shocked that NDSU continues to win (or compete for) National Championships every year. They get our state's top players.

So what is the "potential" that draws a college interest if it's not simply performance within a sport. In my experience it has come down to size, speed, agility/quickness, explosiveness, and lineage. If there is a softball player whose dad played Major League Baseball, or whose mom played Division I softball, and she is decently talented as a player, she will get more attention than a player with similar ability who does not have that lineage. When a prospect who has two parents who played at a high level, this only helps.

Whereas the relationship between college and high school coaches is cordial, a large part of that is because the college coaches need to have the relationship with a high school coach to connect with and evaluate recruits. I'm not convinced that it comes with a ton of respect for the ability of the high school coach to develop talent, (No, I don't feel disrespected, this is just an observation made over years of recruiting insight). To put it bluntly, college coaches believe that they are experts at their craft and can turn the right raw material into the finished product they want. So if the player has the physical traits that successful athletes have at their level, then they can work with the rest.

Try not to let this bother you, but let it answer the question that is associated with this myth of an "apples for apples" comparison with players of your similar (or even inferior) ability. You could absolutely be right and that you are a better player now, and will be in college, than another who is gaining attention. You can't control how the college that offered him or her made that choice and evaluation. Try to not let this frustrate you. At the end of the day, college assistants are retained and promoted, or demoted or let go, based on their ability to get it right in recruiting. If they got it wrong, it will come back to them at a later time, and you probably don't want to be part of a program that regularly gets it wrong. Keep your head up and focus on what you can control.

Myth #4: Camp as much as possible to increase exposure

This is a popular misunderstanding if it's not an overall myth.

Should a player attend a camp in their sport to play in front of the coaches that you want to impress? Absolutely. The power of attending a camp is not a myth nor a misunderstanding. It's the **"as much as possible" myth** that I want to address here. This comes from a simple analogy of fishing – more lines in the water gives you more chances to catch something that you are aiming for. Recruiting doesn't quite work this way.

When a college coach reaches out to a prospective student-athlete, one common opportunity is to invite them to an unofficial visit or a camp that the school is hosting. To visit a school is a good idea – and visiting as many schools that you are interested in is also a good thing. But to attend a camp, where you will be physically participating in your sport, is something you should take into consideration before committing to do so. First, know that camp invitations go out to hundreds of student-athletes. The summer camp is often a way for assistant coaches to make some additional income, and this comes at no cost to the school in terms of getting the opportunity to evaluate you. So the simple invitation to attend a camp is by no means a statement that a school is seriously or heavily interested in you. If you are unclear about this, ask the coach a blunt question to gage their interest. Something to the effect of:

> "Coach, thanks for the camp invite. I'm choosing between camps, and I want to spend my time at schools that are seriously recruiting me. Where am I at on your board?"

You will most likely get a vague answer, but occasionally coaches will respond with a specific question that the coach is looking to answer that could be done at camp. In football, sometimes this is speed, height, or weight. In this situation a coach will say something like, "Our staff loves you, but we need to get an official 40-time." This is a camp that you might want to move up your list. Or in basketball, the response could be, "we want to see how you handle pressure when playing against better competition." Another camp that I would recommend moving up the priority list.

The myth here is the idea that attending camp after camp after camp is a good idea. I think this comes from social media, combined with several "invites". The invitation makes you feel wanted, and the social media posts from others give the appearance that you aren't doing all that you can do. If you've noticed by now, I'm very big on having an **intentional plan** and authentic interactions in the recruiting process. Simply attending camps won't do this.

Now, if you are planning to travel to attend a camp, and there are a few within a short time frame that you can attend, this might be worthwhile. You don't want to make 3 different trips to North Carolina for three different camps, if, over the course of a week you can attend 3 or 4 and knock them all out at once. This is a good move. However, to plan a week of camps in North Carolina, followed by a week in the Midwest, followed by another week in California, would be a bad move.

Also, keep this in mind, nothing is accomplished by simply attending a camp. You have to perform well when you are there. If your performance is off, this can hurt your recruiting. So attending a camp is the proverbial double-edged sword. I had a player one year who attended an FBS camp, and they gave him the specific criteria of wanting to see how fast he was. He ran the fastest 40-yard dash time in camp. He did what they wanted to see. And he did it on an injured knee. However, the injured knee hurt him in some of his position drills because the coaches thought "he didn't move laterally as well as we thought" so the school did not follow through with a scholarship offer. He was a great prospect and still ended up getting a different FBS scholarship, but the camp performance in that instance hurt him more than it helped.

I also bring this up because it is not difficult for an athlete to line up several showcases or camps or tournament opportunities in a row to get in front of several coaches. When an athlete does this, it's fairly likely that their performance will decrease over time, especially when the time between performances is spent traveling and/or sleeping in hotel rooms and eating questionable meals. Again, **the right camps are good, just don't overdo it**.

Another note for this would be if you are looking for the most bang for your buck, check in with different schools who are offering camps and ask them if there will be coaches from other schools at their camps. Many will have this. When they say yes, ask them how many and if they have a list of which schools will be there. I am a much bigger proponent of attending fewer camps with more coaches there to promote exposure than going on a national camping tour after your 10th or 11th grade year.

What about combines? Well, combines are another double-edged sword. If you blow it out of the water on a combine, that can certainly help recruiting, especially if other participants that you out-perform are also being recruited. It's unfortunate that our recruiting world, at least for some schools in schools and sports, has shifted to being heavily reliant on combine type events than the actual playing of a sport. You should also be aware that if you have been telling coaches that you have a 35-inch vertical, and at the combine you post a 26-inch vertical, this will cast doubt on everything else you have told them. When I advise players on combines, I emphasize ones that are **free** (like The Opening offered by Nike) and only after specific combine style training. If you take the risk of going to a combine, make sure it's not a recruiting service in disguise, and prepare for it like you would any athletic event.

Myth #5: Social Media is the Key to Recruiting

Social media is an ever-evolving part of our society, and it can be a useful tool in the recruiting process. This is why I've written an entire chapter on Social Media with tips on how to use it for your benefit in the recruiting process. However, I list this as a myth because it is **NOT** the **KEY** to recruiting, and quite frankly is over-emphasized and overly relied upon by too many student-athletes.

One difficult aspect of Social Media is that it IS a tool used by college coaches. For a time, when coaches were unable to text or call recruits, they were able to message them on Twitter. The rules are ever-changing, so I'm not going to breakdown the NCAA rules about Social Media communication (just keep in mind, as the athlete you can't do anything wrong with this). But as college coaches made Twitter a regular tool to message athletes, as well as promoting their college program, the response from student-athletes has moved to almost conducting (and therefore broadcasting) their recruiting experience through Social Media.

Athletes should know that coaches who are interested in them will take a deep dive into their social media if there are any concerns about who you are. In a world where your social media can depict anything you choose to allow, it is a major red flag when a prospect's social media accounts suggest (or promote) questionable to negative behavior and/or comments. So while many athletes want the coaches to be impressed by their posts of highlight films or competing experiences or offers from other schools, they neglect the reality that the same account might lead some schools to move on from their recruitment.

Another reason why this is a myth is that what might appear to be an intriguing social media account to the average person can come across like an oversell to the college coach. The basic idea here is that "talent speaks for itself" and if you have to oversell your social media promotion – like slow motion video of you working out – means that you need to dress up average talent to make it appear to be above-average talent. I will talk about the right way to approach social media later. For now, don't buy into the myth that the best Instagram and Twitter accounts drive the most aggressive recruiting opportunities.

Final Thoughts

The recruiting process requires both optimism and skepticism. One of the best ways to have both is to be aware of the myths that often accompany recruiting. They will be attractive, and they can motivate you (either player or parent) into decisions that seem right for the time but actually have negative effects. The rest of this book will help you navigate the process the right way, and if one of these myths is pulling you in a different direction than the path outlined, resist that urge.

5 SNAKES: RECRUITING SERVICES

Repeat this: **DO NOT PAY FOR A RECRUITING SERVICE.**

When a friend tells you about how they signed up for a recruiting service, and now their child has a profile page on a national database... **DO NOT PAY FOR A RECRUITING SERVICE.**

When you see a social media post from a company claiming to have "bridged the gap" or paved the way for a blue chip athlete to sign with a Division I school... **DO NOT PAY FOR A RECRUITING SERVICE.**

I don't care if a service promises to set you up at dinner with Anson Dorrance, Nick Saban, John Calipari, or Muffet McGraw... **DO NOT PAY FOR A RECRUITING SERVICE.**

   In my experience, recruiting services do the complete opposite of what you think they will do for you as a prospective student athlete. You think they will get your "profile" or information into the hands of the colleges you want to notice you, but in reality they sent out massive database information that very few schools will even look at. They may claim to connect you with the coach of your dreams. When the truth is that those coaches I mentioned above are meeting with you for one primary reason: They think you can play at their level and help them win. Guess what? You don't need a recruiting service for them to "discover" you, and those high profile coaches don't have any interest in talking to a recruiting service. These services promise to help you navigate this process, but in reality they just muddy the waters and you will have difficulty telling what is genuine interest from auto-generated mailers and emails.

Now, there are both paid and "free" recruiting services available. In this chapter I'm focusing on issuing a stern warning against utilizing a recruiting service that you have to pay for. This does not mean that I am in favor of a free service, nor do I think it's "harmless." Some free recruiting services only offer their "free" service for a base package, and then seek to convince you to upgrade for a fee. This is the classic foot-in-the-door technique. Don't fall for it. Even if the service is truly free (which doesn't make economic sense), they are likely to (at best) get your name, email, and address on other databases (if they sell your information) or to some random schools which will send you a flyer for their camp or possibly a brochure about their school. Some people like this attention. Keep in mind, you can probably go online **to a school you are actually interested in**, fill out an online form, and be put on the mailing list to receive the same information. Ultimately, even if it's free, why would you give a random business your personal information when they can't deliver anything you could (more clearly and accurately) do yourself?

I believe that recruiting services are **SNAKES** that at best have no real impact on recruiting, but at worst (which in my experience is the norm) promise a lot for a substantial fee, only to blame your high school coach, club coach, or school counselor when these lofty promises fall flat. Recruiting does not need a third party, and recruiting services have had to create a problem for which they claim to be the solution. As mentioned earlier, because the previous two generations could have capable college athletes fall through the cracks, recruiting services play off of this historical, not current, problem. They exploit a parent's vulnerability both in their love for their child and their enhanced opinion of their child's ability. If you are a parent and think your child is under-represented by his or her high school or club coach, **still do not turn to a recruiting service**. You are exactly the audience they look for, and I have NEVER had a player that felt this way and turned to a recruiting service find better opportunities than I (the coach) was able to generate. There is nothing wrong with taking a more proactive approach with your recruiting, and I strongly believe this starts with a conversation with your respective coach. Just do NOT think that some random third party service somehow has greater insight or connections. They do not, but they will be happy to take your money.

I have a few stories about recruiting services that I would like to share, and then I will end with some common sense understandings which will reinforce why investing in a recruiting service is counterproductive and expensive. If you paid for this book, this chapter alone could save you thousands of dollars.

Story 1: "The Gap"

The 2005 football season was my first as a head coach. Not only that, but I had moved from Minnesota to the state of Virginia in the middle of June to take over a program. The previous staff had been successful, and they moved as an entire staff to a newly built school. So when I took over, I had to hire a staff of people with whom I had never worked, and I had to hit the ground running to build relationships and get to know my team. The first day of practice was August 1. Needless to say, the senior class I was inheriting was a class in transition, and I didn't want them to feel like they got a raw deal. I had seen game film from the previous two years, and I got to know these young men as quickly and as strongly as I could in a short time.

Both during and after our season, I was active in helping my seniors (and juniors) with their recruiting process. However, as a new coach in a new part of the country, I was meeting many of the college coaches for the first time. I had one senior player who had good size and speed, and he was an All-District Honorable Mention player. He was good but not great. Because of my being new, his family paid a recruiting service roughly $3,000 to "help" him get more exposure. I warned against this, and every coach that came through commented to me that they didn't do anything with any of the services. I had a couple of Division II schools interested in him, but that particular conference was very limited on scholarships allotted to each school, so most of their players were on little to no athletic scholarship money. Through their interactions with me, they met my player, and he went on some visits. He was ultimately offered a PWO (preferred walk on) spot at a school, so there was no athletic scholarship given to this player. The recruiting service claimed that they got him an "offer" – notice they are implying he got a football scholarship although there was no athletic money here – simply because his name was on a list that they emailed to dozens of schools (along with a bunch of other names). The very coaches from that school told me they didn't have anything to do with receiving the "reports" from the recruiting service. Long story short, I understood why his family felt the need to fill in the gap between a change in coaching staffs so their player wouldn't be at a disadvantage. However, they ultimately shelled out about $3,000 more than what I did for free (and more aggressively and with greater knowledge of the player and access to conversations with college coaches) to end up with the opportunity that he got.

Story 2: The Camp

This story could be a chapter in and of itself, but I will keep it focused on the recruiting service. Just a couple of years ago our school hosted a "national" football camp that conducts itself in various locations throughout the country. The camp is a significant investment for participants, and the camp itself claims to be a pathway to being a great football player including earning scholarships. Again, my focus is not on the camp for this as much as the recruiting service they partnered with. This service paid the camp a substantial fee to not only be a vendor at their camp locations, but to present to the parents (and sometimes athletes) during the course of the camp. The message was simple – if you want to have the advantage in recruiting, you need to use our service to give yourself the best chances to be seen and offered by colleges.

Since I've given presentations about recruiting every year, I was not worried about my student-athletes falling for this scheme. Yet as the parents (who already shelled out hundreds of dollars for their child to participate in camp) sat there listening to the presentation, you could see the combination of guilt and aspiration. In their minds, signing up for this recruiting service was essential for their child to have an opportunity. This couldn't be further from the truth. I literally heard one of the two salesmen from the recruiting service tell the mother of a 6th grader: "You should really get on this and get his profile page up for the colleges to start to see. We would hate to see him get behind the other kids in his class." Are you kidding me? A 6th grade football player? I hope this makes you as angry as it made me. This line is total bullshit, and you need to know it. Not just because he's a 6th grader, but because there's not a single profile page in the country that will put you further ahead or further behind others.

At this same camp, an assistant coach from a Big 12 (FBS) school was present because his 8th grade son wanted to participate in the camp. He spent a large part of the camp talking to me, and after we heard the sales pitch from the recruiting service, we decided to turn up the heat. He told me that he has never seen nor used any report from a recruiting service, and that he's never talked to anyone from this service (nor would he). His perspective was simple and true: "If I think a kid can play, I'm going to talk to his high school coach, watch his film, and size him up in person." So with this in mind, I went over and talked to the sales rep and asked about a hypothetical player who wanted to be noticed by this particular Big 12 school. The rep had no idea that the man next to me was on staff at that school. The rep stated "oh yeah, we do a lot of work with them." I asked him to name which coach he worked with, and he couldn't name a single coach on staff. Not one. So I asked to give me a staff with which they work closely, and he named a Big 10 coaching staff that I happen to know fairly well. When I started rattling off names for him to tell me who he worked with – so that I could verify the service through them – the sales rep quickly bailed and said something to the effect of "well I'd need to check my contact list which I don't have with me today to let you know. We work with so many schools that it's hard to keep them straight." Keep in mind, I let him choose the school that he said would attest to the work they did as a recruiting service. He couldn't name one coach at the one school he thought would be an advocate for them. **This is a sham**. And this is one of the most popular, national recruiting services.

Story 3: The Truth Bomb

A few years ago I had a talented quarterback, who because of his ability got to participate in a national quarterback competition series.

I not only supported him participating, but I helped get him the invitation because the event was free and sponsored by a major athletic apparel company. To me, these free events are great to compete against the best, but I warned him against any of the vendors and services that might be "partners". He traveled to Florida to compete in the event, and it was a good experience.

The event, however, must have shared his contact information with a recruiting service. This service then reached out to his father to promote their services. Luckily his father had heard my recruiting presentation twice, and he was on alert when he received the call. The sales rep for the recruiting service asked how many "Division I scholarship offers" his son had. The father replied that his son had none. The rep feigned being appalled at that answer and told the father that his son was "way behind" in the recruiting process, and that "he should have 10 to 20 offers by this point" (it was the spring of his junior year). Without missing a beat, my QB's father replied with "OK, tell me how many quarterbacks in the state of Minnesota have division I offers?" There was silence on the other end. The answer was that there was one quarterback, a year behind my QB at a different school, that had a Division I offer. Otherwise there weren't any.

The sales rep said that he'd have to look in to that but that he had coaches lined up to evaluate my quarterback. Knowing he wasn't going to bite, but wanted to find out the cost, my QB's father pretended to play along. The cost was "a few thousand."

The father was relaying this story to me at a baseball game, and he mentioned that a certain Mountain West (FBS) school was one of the schools that was eagerly awaiting the chance to evaluate my QB. Well, that college's very Quarterbacks coach was AT the baseball game (evaluating an athlete from the opposing team). I had been talking to him about my QB, and they had already evaluated him and he probably wasn't a fit for their school. This was something that I knew and respected through my authentic communication with the coach. So I asked him about the recruiting service. He told me that he has nothing to do with them, and that "a lot of groups" send them files or pages of reports, but he doesn't know if anyone on staff ever even looks at them. This was another example of a recruiting service making either loose associations or flat out false claims to take advantage of a parent's love and ambition for their child.

Use Common Sense – Step Back from Your Emotions & Understand the Process

For most, if not all sports, the recruiting process is going to culminate in the college coach talking to the high school or club coach, meeting the recruit and his or her family, visiting campus, and then extending the offer. None of those steps require or involve a third party recruiting service. If the college coach that you want to play for is going to need to talk to your high school coach, either you or your coach can make that happen. And you can do it more quickly and with greater clarity than allowing a recruiting service to act as your agent. In addition, I can attest that high school coaches and college coaches are not going to work through a service to connect with each other. Cut out the middle man and don't give them access to your information or your money.

Also understand this – **you are not going to trick your way into a scholarship**. Recruiting is chaotic and confusing, but some will enlist the services out of the belief that they can somehow present you in the best light, or possibly better than you actually are. While there are definitely some scholarship offers extended each year that don't make sense to me, they are not the result of tricking the college into the offer. For whatever reason, that college saw something they think can make their team better, and they chose to offer. But please don't believe that a service or a middle man has some secret access or magic to make this happen.

Both players and parents should approach references to past successes with a great dose of skepticism. For example, one of the years that the previously mentioned football camp was hosted at our school also happened to be the year that I had one of the top football prospects in the state of Minnesota. The camp virtually begged me to have my player attend, for free, at least one of the on-field sessions. In addition, the recruiting service offered to make him a free profile. He turned it down (having been cautioned against this many times), but he did attend a free session of the camp. I'm sure the camp took photos, filmed him in a drill, and will boast of having one of their campers having earned a major FBS scholarship. Had he agreed to the free profile page, the recruiting service would have used him as an example of getting one of their clients a major offer. He had over a dozen FBS offers well before and without any connection to the camp or the recruiting service. But the camp and the service would have been happy to associate their product with his success, marketing it to players and parents as the reverse relationship (that his participation in camp got him the scholarships).

Finally, please also approach the "help wanted" posts and emails with a great deal of skepticism. Every year, sometimes more than once, I will get a text or an email from a recruiting service that says "I just got an email that an FCS school needs one more WR to fill their recruiting class. This is a scholarship spot. Email (or text) me back with your player's info." Again, total BS. Recruiting from the college perspective involves doing one's research, visiting schools and watching film, talking with coaches, and having kids out for a visit. Schools will start with hundreds of potential student athletes, and narrow that down to the ones they think could play at their school, and then they prioritize those in order of who they want the most. To think that a school has an opening, and that none of the (in this example) receivers they wanted chose them, that they just throw their arms up and say "I don't know who else is out there" is complete garbage.

I've been on the high school end of this scenario two times. But there was no recruiting service involved at all. Two different teams (one FBS and one FCS) came out of spring football with injuries or transfers that created a need. Because the assistant coach who had visited my school had my player on their list already from an earlier meeting with me, they simply called me to see if my player was unsigned. When he was, they showed up at my school within the next 24 hours with the National Letter of Intent to sign. So yes, roster spots open up. No, they aren't filled by some third party recruiting service. They are filled through potential player lists kept by each college in their recruiting "board" and through the availability as communicated with the player or high school coach. No room and no need for a recruiting service here.

Final Thoughts

For both players and parents, **understand your vulnerability** in wanting the best opportunity and situation. Recruiting services have no value in this process. There's nothing they can do, despite what they promise, that you and/or your coach cannot do on your own. We've already addressed the myth of "falling through the cracks" and even if that was the truth, somebody who has never coached you is not the answer. Be aware that "free" is simply a means to get their foot in the door, or to gain access to sell your information. College coaches do not actively use recruiting services. Sure, the services blast out emails or mail lengthy database reports to schools, but does anyone even look at them? The only schools to which this could be mildly helpful would be very small, non-scholarship schools who don't have the personnel resources to cover comprehensive recruiting. However, these are also the schools that if you are interested in, you can easily reach out to and they will likely be immediately interested in you. So why not be the one to control your process? Do you really want an email from a tiny Division III school in New Mexico that you have no intention of even considering? Please do not run the risk of missing opportunities because you are trusting a person or a service that does not actually have the access they claim to. Be smarter than that, and don't suffer from a case of imagined FOMO (Fear of Missing Out). That's not how recruiting works. Focus on the later parts of this book and you will have a clear path on how to put your best foot forward in this process.

6 ELIGIBILITY REQUIREMENTS

Just as you are a student-athlete in high school, with the priority of being a "student" first, the same thing applies in college. Whereas you might be choosing a school primarily because of the opportunity to play your sport there, you will still need to "qualify" to be a student at your chosen school. In addition, your continued eligibility will come with academic performance expectations. This chapter is going to focus on what is called the "initial eligibility" meaning what is required in order for you to be eligible to play your sport upon enrolling at a school and arriving on campus.

NCAA Eligibility Center

If you are considering (or want to be considered by) a Division I or Division II school, you need to have registered with the NCAA Eligibility Center. You can search for this website through a simple Google search, or you can type in the URL: **www.eligibilitycenter.org**. This is a mandatory step for any Division I or Division II athlete.

In simple terms, the Eligibility Center is a branch of the National Collegiate Athletic Association (NCAA) that verifies the academic performance of a prospective student-athlete. To create an account will cost $90 at the time of this writing. This is something that must be paid in order for the Eligibility Center to evaluate and verify your standing in order to be initially eligible to participate at your chosen

Division I or Division II school. In addition, you will need to be registered before a school can offer you an official visit.

If you register with the Eligibility Center, your school will need to send your transcript, and you will want to have your ACT or SAT test scores sent to the Eligibility Center. Enter the NCAA code on either test to have your scores sent directly to the Eligibility Center. The code is **9999** on both the ACT and the SAT. Make sure you select this option when taking the test.

The Eligibility Center will not mark a student-athlete as qualifying until he or she has graduated from high school. It is only once proof of graduation has been received, usually in the form of a final transcript from one's school, will your status change to be ELIGIBLE if you have met the initial eligibility requirements for your Division of play. Do not be alarmed if you check on your account throughout high school and it says you are currently ineligible – again, this is because the Eligibility Center is still waiting for your final transcript.

If you know that you are not interested in Division I or Division II schools, and you want to focus on playing your sport at the Division III level, you do not need to create an account and register with the Eligibility Center. The NCAA offers a free "profile page" that will also connect you with email updates, but this is not necessary. It is harmless, but I don't usually recommend this to my Division III student-athletes. In most cases, my athletes that want to play at Division III schools have a few specific ones in mind, and we will contact those schools directly.

Core Grade Point Average

The NCAA, for eligibility purposes, only deals with the CORE GPA of potential student-athletes. The purpose for this is to provide as close to a standard expectation as possible across an educational landscape that features different academic tracks, course offerings, grading scales, and credit definitions.

A core course is an NCAA-approved, year-long credit of English, Mathematics, Science, Social Studies, or Foreign Language. While most core classes offered at a high school can be counted by the Eligibility Center, I strongly to encourage you (or you through the help of a school counselor) to make sure they are NCAA approved. If you enter a Google search of "List of NCAA Courses" the first link will take you to the NCAA portal that can let you search for your school, and then search "All Approved Courses". Again, the best way to be sure that the classes you have taken are NCAA approved is to meet with your school counselor, look at your schedule and transcript, and compare this to the NCAA resource about your specific school's offering.

The NCAA calculates your Core GPA based on 16 Core courses. Later in this chapter I will outline the differing requirements between Division I and Division II. However, in either Division, the Core GPA is calculated through the assigning of points to a **year** credit. This is important to understand – for the NCAA calculation, they require 16 full years of credits to be earned. If you are a semester school, and your school gives one credit per semester (for example, a year of US History earns you 2 credits at your high school), the NCAA would consider your full year of a course to be a single credit. You are allowed to combine semesters, quarters, or trimester final grades to equal a single year credit, and I will show you how to determine the GPA if you have to do this.

The NCAA will use the term "quality points" to evaluate your Core GPA. Please note that there is no advantage for having taken AP or Honors courses, and the Core GPA does not take into consideration a weighted grading scale. An "A" is an "A" whether you took regular US History or AP US History - they are the same in the eyes of the NCAA Core GPA calculations. The Eligibility Center also does not concern itself with a "+" or "-". A "B+" and a "B" and a "B-" are all considered a "B" by the NCAA. The point values are as follows:

A = 4 quality points
B = 3 quality points
C = 2 quality points
D = 1 quality point

Core GPA is calculated by adding up all of the quality points earned for the 16 required courses, and then that sum is divided by 16.

For a full-year course with a single grade at the end of the term, this is a very straight forward calculation: the grade earned gives you the quality points associated with the letter grade.

If you have semester courses that issue a final semester grade, you would take the quality points for each semester grade, and divide them by two for the value of the year credit. For example, if you received a B+ for your first semester of US History, and then an A for your second semester, you would add 3 (for the B) to 4 (for the A) and then divide by 2 (the number of terms in the year). This would make your year credit of US History carry 3.5 quality points.

Note: many people would think that if you average a B+ and an A that the median grade is an A-, therefore earning 4 quality points. This is incorrect. **Whatever terms are reported on your transcript will be what is used in calculating your quality points.**

If you are on trimesters, you would follow the same logic. You would take your three trimester grades, add up those quality points, and then divide by three. For our hypothetical US History course, say a prospective student-athlete earned an A first trimester, followed by a C in both the second and third trimester. The total quality points would be 4 + 2 + 2 to give us 8, and then we would need to divide it by 3 (the number of trimesters) which will give us 2.666 quality points.

If you need to combine courses to get to a full year's worth of credits, you would follow the same breakdown outlined above, as long as the courses are Core courses. For example, if you earned an A in Economics for a semester, and a C in Political Science, that would work out to 3 quality points (4+2=6, divided by 2 terms).

Finally, when determining Core GPA, I always want prospective student-athletes to be aware that the NCAA is going to look at your best 16 Core classes as long as you meet the required number of each category. So at the school where I currently teach at, we offer several Social Studies and English elective courses. If one of my student-athletes took a difficult course like AP Human Geography and got a C, only later to take Sociology, Psychology, and Criminology and got an A in all of them, then they can "replace" that C with the A. This can only be done if the student-athlete has more core courses than they need. This is an easy thing to consider – if a high school student takes Math, English, Science, and Social Studies every year (for a year), then any Foreign Language or other core department elective will be additional core courses to choose from.

If you have taken a class "pass/fail" or been granted a credit through a non-graded credit recovery (make up) program, the NCAA will consider an earned credit, without a standard letter grade, to be a D in determining quality points.

ACT and SAT Scores

In addition to your Core GPA, the NCAA will evaluate your initial eligibility through a national standardized test – either the ACT or the SAT. While any student-athlete anywhere can sign up to take either test, the ACT tends to be more popular in the Midwest region, while the SAT is more prevalent on the East and West coasts. Both tests are offered throughout the country, and depending up on your situation, you may want to consider taking both tests at least one time. Otherwise, plan on taking the test that is popular in your area at least twice.

Test scores are used on an inverse sliding scale in combination with your Core GPA. The higher one's Core GPA, the lower the SAT or ACT score needs to be in order to qualify. Scores are recorded as the sum of all four parts of the test. For example, with the ACT, if a student-athlete scores a 20 in English, a 20 in Reading, a 20 in Math, and a 20 in Science would be scored by the NCAA as an 80. The composite score that you would receive would tell you the score you received on each of the four parts individually, but then would give you an average "composite" score. In this example, your composite ACT score would be a 20. For NCAA purposes, look at each part. SAT scores are reported as an overall cumulative score. So scoring a 220 on each of the four parts would be reported as an SAT score of 880.

The NCAA will combine multiple test attempts to create a "Super Score" that allows you to take your best segment score from different tests and put them together. From my ACT example above, if that student took the ACT a second time and scored a 24 in English, 22 in Reading, but dropped to an 18 in Math and a 16 in Science. The overall score of this second test would still be an 80, **but** this student-athlete would have his test **Super Scored** to include the 24 in English, 22 in Reading, and then keep the 20 in Math and 20 in

Science. This would increase his overall ACT score (for NCAA Eligibility purposes) to an 86, up 6 points from the first attempt. The same scenario works for the SAT.

Should you take the ACT or the SAT? That is a question that I would recommend you talk to your school counselor about, and measure the answer against where you think you stand with your Core GPA. If you have a high Core GPA and simply need to get an average score to qualify, then either test will be fine. However, your academic skills and strengths may point you towards performing better on one standard test as compared to another. Your counselor would be the best place to start in determining which test is best for you.

The Guide For The College Bound Student-Athlete

The best eligibility resource to have on hand is the *"Guide for the College Bound Student Athlete"* put together each year by the NCAA. It can be downloaded or accessed for free through the NCAA website: **www.ncaa.org/student-athletes/future**. For younger high school athletes, I recommend printing or saving a copy of this each year and referring to it if questions arise. Within this guide is a worksheet for initial eligibility for Division I and Division II, and a copy of the sliding scale. The requirements are different for Division I and Division II student-athletes.

Division I Eligibility

To be initially eligible to play Division I sports, a student-athlete must graduate and have earned 16 year credits in the following Core Course categories:
    4 years of English
    3 years of Math
    2 years of Natural/Physical Science
    1 year of an additional English, Math, Natural/Physical Science
    2 years of Social Science (Social Studies)

4 years of additional Core courses

Division I Sliding Scale: The lowest initial eligibility Core GPA is a 2.300 which would require a 980 on the SAT or a 75 on the ACT. If you have a 3.500 Core GPA or better, your lowest SAT score must be a 400, or an ACT of 37. The higher your test score, the lower your Core GPA can be.

The NCAA requires you to "lock in" ten of the Core Course credits before the start of a student-athletes senior year. Seven of these ten courses must be English, Math, or Science. If you complete the Division I worksheet, this is what the "**10/7**" indication is referring to. A student-athlete can complete courses during the summer before their senior year begins and these courses can then count within their 10 locked courses. However, if you took extra courses during your senior year, these could not override the 10 courses you had to lock when you started your senior year.

I strongly recommend that you print either the entire *Guide For College Bound Student-Athletes* or at least print the Division I (or Division II) worksheets and fill them out as you plan your high school workload.

For Division I, you will fall into one of the following categories: **Early Academic Qualifier, Qualifier, Academic Redshirt,** or **Nonqualifier.**

Both the **Early Academic Qualifier** and the **Qualifier** will be fully eligible to participate when you enroll as a full-time student. The difference between these two is that certain requirements (see the *Guide* mentioned above) can allow students to enroll and compete after only three years of high school. A popular example of this would be the football players who leave their high school a semester early to enroll at their college and participate in spring football practices. In order to be an Early Academic Qualifier, the Core GPA and test score requirements are higher than what is needed to be a Qualifier.

An **Academic Redshirt** certification will allow you to receive a scholarship and practice with your team, but you cannot compete during your first semester of being a full-time student at your school. There will be credit requirements during that first semester which will determine your academic eligibility for the following semester. If these academic requirements are met, you will be eligible to compete with your team starting with your second year at the school.

A **Nonqualifier** is exactly as it sounds – you do not qualify for a scholarship and you cannot practice or compete with your team during your first year at your school. You can still enroll if you can gain admission. If you go this route, be sure to talk to the coach and an academic counselor within the athletic department to make sure that the courses you take during this year of being a nonqualifier will set you up to become eligible to play the next year. Many student-athletes who are nonqualifiers will choose to attend a Junior College or a Prep School to improve their academic standing before transferring or enrolling in a four-year college.

Division II Eligibility

At first glance, Division II eligibility looks very similar to the Division I eligibility standards. I would not say that it is "easier" to qualify at a Division II school, but there is greater flexibility in how you can become eligible at a Division II school. You will still need to earn 16 year credits in Core Courses. However, the quantity needed varies from Division I requirements, and there is no "10/7" rule at the Division II level. This means that while I do not recommend that you load your schedule with core courses your senior year, if you need to do this to qualify, it is possible at the Division II level.

Core Course category requirements for Division II:
3 years of English
2 years of Math
2 years of Natural/Physical Sicence
3 additional years of English, Math, or Natural/Physical Science
2 years of Social Science
4 additional years of Core courses

Division II offers a **Full Qualifier Sliding Scale** and a **Partial Qualifier Sliding Scale**. To be a **Full Qualifier**, the minimum ACT is a 37, and the minimum SAT is a 400, if you have a 3.300 or better Core GPA. The minimum Core GPA to be a Full Qualifier is a 2.200, which will then require a 70 or better on the ACT or a 920 on the SAT.

In terms of being a Partial Qualifier, the minimum ACT is a 37, and the minimum SAT is a 400, to go along with a 3.050-3.299 Core GPA. The minimum Core GPA to be a Partial Qualifier is a 2.000, and it requires a 900 SAT or a 68 or better ACT.

The certification categories for Division II are the same as Division I except you would replace the term "Academic Redshirt" with "Partial Qualifier". If you are a Division II Partial Qualifier, you will be able to receive a scholarship and practice with the team during your first year of enrollment, but you will not be able to compete. If you meet certain academic requirements your first year in school, you will be able to compete starting your second year of enrollment.

Division III

Division III schools do not work from the same initial eligibility framework as Division I or Division II schools. Because Division III schools do not offer athletic scholarships, they are not part of the Eligibility Center certification process.

The basic understanding for Division III schools is that if a student-athlete is admitted as a full-time student, then he or she is eligible to participate in sports right away.

Now, this is up to the discretion of each individual school. As you explore Division III schools, I strongly advise you to work with the college coach and a counselor from within the athletic department to make sure that you will be eligible for immediate participation. It is possible that individual schools may have academic parameters in place for initial eligibility to participate. So while this is not something uniformly regulated by the NCAA at the Division III level, know that individual schools have their own discretion to determine initial eligibility.

Final Thoughts

Don't let this information feel overwhelming. There are a few practical actions steps that you can take to feel in control of your own eligibility:

1. Go to the link provided and print the Guide for College-Bound Student-Athletes
2. Set a plan for when you want to take either the SAT or the ACT. Plan out two test dates in advance and register for them.
3. Talk to your high school counselor and inform him/her that you want to play your sport in college and you need to make sure you are taking the right courses.
4. Treat your academic work like you would treat your training regimen – both will empower your opportunities and success at the college level.

In the next chapter I will outline the Academic Plan (Chapter 7), followed by a chapter on the Timeline (Chapter 8). This should not be a source of stress, but rather one of empowerment. Once you know the plan and the timing, all you need to do is follow through with the actions and behaviors required. When this happens, along with performing in the classroom, initial eligibility is never a problem.

7 THE ACADEMIC PLAN

The Academic Plan is a simple process, yet it will need to involve conversations at home and with your school counselor. This is not a "one size fits all" plan, and your own academic strengths, weaknesses, and school situation will influence the plan.

Regular vs. Honors/AP Courses

The politically correct advice in this conversation is to challenge you to stretch yourself academically. As a teacher and a coach, I would agree. Growth comes through persevering through adversity and reaching levels that were demanded challenges to reach. However, at the same time, in counseling you about NCAA Eligibility, you need to understand that the NCAA does not care about the level of your Core Courses. What I mean by this is something I said earlier: An A is an A, a B is a B, a C is a C, and a D is a D in the eyes of the NCAA. They do not weight grades or give you bonus points for taking academically challenging courses. Through this lens, it would make more sense to get an A- in Biology than it would to get a C+ in AP Biology. Again, I am not advising this as a blanket rule, but this is something of which you should be aware.

Now, if you are a strong student and getting a final grade in a course below a B- is very rare, whether or not it is an Honors or AP course, then you don't need to worry about this consideration. Take whatever courses you want. **The basic achievement goal of The Academic Plan is simple: B- or better in every Core Course.** If you can do that, then this really is not something to worry about.

The concern is for the student-athlete who is capable of taking the higher level course but is likely to receive a C+ or below in the higher level course. The difference between a C+ and a B- in the eyes of the NCAA is significant. I am not saying that you should not take an advanced course. Advanced courses will prepare you for the more rigorous content that you will be engaging with in college courses. However, I would recommend a thoughtful approach to selecting your courses.

If you want to take higher level courses in high school, ask yourself the following questions:

(1) Do I enjoy or have an interest in the subject or topic?
(2) Will I have the time (and follow-through) to complete the coursework?
(3) Do I have the resources necessary to be successful in this course?

If you can answer yes to all three of those questions, this is a higher level course that you should take. Even if you get a C+ or worse, it can be valuable for your academic growth. If you answer no to any of those questions, then I recommend avoiding the course because success becomes more unlikely without these three pillars in place.

When should you become concerned about this? If you have taken a number of higher level courses, and your school uses a weighted grading system, there may be a significant discrepancy between your NCAA Core GPA and your high school cumulative GPA. For example, a student who has taken several AP or Honors Core Courses and received mostly C or C+ grades, his or her cumulative school GPA can be at or above a 3.0. However, because the C's all equate to two quality points, their NCAA Core GPA may be closer to a 2.0. This is why it is important to both know what Core Courses are and to focus on the basic goal of "**B- or better**" in all of them.

How Many Core Courses To Take

An easy way to set yourself up for academic success is what I call a 4x4 plan. This ensures that you will have 16 Core credits upon graduation. The 4x4 plan is to take English, Math, Science, and Social Studies for the entire year, all four years of high school. As long as you earn each credit, this is a foolproof way to make sure you aren't short on Core Credits as you hit your senior year of high school.

In addition, any Foreign Language or Core electives that you take will count as Core Courses. The average high school student will take two years of a language, and at least one year of Core electives. In this typical situation, if the student also had a 4x4 plan, that would give him 19 Core credits. Given the NCAA will evaluate the best 16 (given you meet the minimum number of credits in each category). This would give this student the flexibility to replace three credits with other core courses in order to utilize the best possible Core GPA.

This does not mean that you should focus only on Core Courses during high school. Many non-Core Courses are available at most schools, and often these are enjoyable courses. These include physical education, fine arts, music, and FACS classes. Not all electives within a Core department will count as Core Courses, including most "independent study" courses. Again, check the NCAA approved course list for your school to determine whether or not a course will count as a Core Course. Balance is key in all areas of life, including your academic work in high school. It is perfectly fine to take some courses that you enjoy even if they are not a Core Course. At the same time, beware of stacking your schedule with non-Core Courses or setting up a "slide" – a schedule which lacks challenging or core courses intended to reduce or eliminate your workload at the end of your senior year.

Many times your school's requirements for graduation will not have the same requirements as the NCAA. So while you will need to graduate in order to be eligible, you could very well graduate but not have the proper amount of Core courses. Again, meet with your school counselor and reference either this book or the NCAA worksheet to make sure you are taking the right classes.

Middle School Credits That Count

It is possible for some credits earned in Middle School to be counted towards NCAA Eligibility. While they will most likely not count towards your high school GPA, you will receive high school credit. The most common areas in which I have seen this happen is with a Foreign Language (i.e. Spanish I) and Math (Algebra, Geometry). For example, at my school it is common for students to have taken Algebra in 7th grade, and then in 8th grade they have taken Geometry and Spanish I. They start their high school schedule with Algebra 2 and Spanish II. This gives them 3 years of Core Credits (in the eyes of the NCAA) upon entering high school. If this has been your experience, you will need to reference the NCAA approved courses for your school and work through your school counselor to see if your middle school credits can count for high school and the NCAA. If this has happened, this can add increased flexibility in the high school schedule.

The Home School Student

If you are a home school student, this does not prevent you from participating in your sport or achieving initial eligibility certification from the NCAA. I recommend that you go over the Home School segment in the *Guide for the College Bound Student-Athlete*. If you have questions about how to make sure that you are meeting these requirements, you will need to contact the NCAA directly. Start this process early, even if you are not completely sure that you want to play in college. There may be additional steps you need to take, and you will want to be aware of that as you progress through your home school education.

Students with Learning Disabilities

Documented learning disabilities can have an effect on initial eligibility standards, including having the eligibility standards modified for you. However, this is not guaranteed. There are specific steps you will need to take, and you may need to reach out to the NCAA directly. Do not assume that because you received accommodations and/or modifications in high school that this will bypass the Eligibility Center standards. You can find some information about this in the *Guide for the College Bound Student-Athlete*.

The Plan

If you are looking for a place to start, you can use this plan as template. This is not inflexible, and I realize that at the time of reading this book, you may be well into your high school career. It is likely that your experience will overlap significantly with this suggested plan, and don't panic if there are gaps between your transcript and what is outlined below. However, be cognizant of the Core Course requirements and your future scheduling.

9th Grade   English, Math, Science, Social Studies, & Language
10th Grade English, Math, Science, Social Studies, & Language
11th Grade English, Math, Science, Social Studies
12th Grade English, Math OR Science, Social Studies

This will get you a minimum of 17 Core Courses during your high school career, and it also gives you flexibility during your Junior and Senior year.

This plan can vary depending upon whether or not you earned Core credits in Middle School, and if your interested field of study includes Core electives. For example, if you know that you want to be a writer, so your open spots in your Junior and Senior year are filled with English electives that count as NCAA Core Courses, then you might not need to take non-graduation required Core electives in other areas.

Online Courses

The prevalence of high school students taking online courses has seen a surge of interest in recent years. Many students enjoy the freedom, and the perceived easier grading, that an online course provides. Different states have varying legislation on the availability of online courses for high school students. My advice: **BEWARE of Online Courses**.

I'm sure that there are some situations in which an online class will be beneficial to you as a student-athlete. When online courses first became available, they were difficult to pass. Not because the content was difficult, but because the high school student often was not equipped with the time-management skills (nor the discipline) to pace themselves to be successful. Before you take an online course, it will be your responsibility to make sure that the online course (if you expect it to be an NCAA approved Core Course) is actually NCAA approved. Each online course platform is different, so take the effort to look into this. What you would hate is to take an online course expecting it to count, only to find out after the course is completed that it was not NCAA approved.

Finally, ask yourself WHY you are taking an online course. If it is because (a) you don't want to have to go to a traditional class every day, or (b) it sounds like an easier option, or (c) you don't like the classroom teacher, I need to be honest in saying that these are not valid reasons. Having to work through difficult situations or do more difficult course work will prepare you for college. Simply moving to the easiest path possible is not a choice that will empower growth. If you are taking the course because (a) it is not offered at your school, or (b) you want to take some online courses in college so this is a preparation for that, then you have a more realistic mindset and reason for taking an online course.

Final Thoughts

Don't fret about the Academic Plan. Just be aware. Take courses that will challenge you, but balance those courses with Core Courses in which you can earn good grades. Remember two basic principles: **B- or Better** and the basic **4x4 Core Plan**. Again, these are not absolute, but if you keep both principals in mind, you will be moving in the right direction.

8 THE TIMELINE

As with any journey, utilizing a timeline will help keep you on pace, moving forward, and in the chaos of recruiting, a semblance of stability.

Before I outline the timeline, please know that **this is a recommendation**. It is quite possible that you are reading this book, or entering the recruiting process, at any point along this timeline. This does not mean that you are behind, or that there are gaps in your recruiting journey. What it does mean is that you may need to compress the space between events, and make sure that you do not neglect a necessary step within the timeline. There may be some steps that you have already taken and not realized, or possibly steps that you have missed that are inconsequential. Again, please use this as a guide.

Stage One: Before Entering High School

If, as a middle schooler, you believe that you might want to participate in collegiate sports after high school, go through this book and make mental notes of important points. Focus on things like being a great teammate, your training regimen, and your academic performance. Go into your high school experience with your eyes open focused on the steps you will need to take to be successful.

Also in this stage, registering for your 9th grade year will take place during your 8th grade school year. Think about Core Courses when registering. If you started Core Courses in Middle School, know that those grades matter, and continue with them as you enter high school.

The last important step in this stage is to start to connect with your high school program in whatever ways are available. If this means attending games in the sport that you like, attending camps offered by the high school, training with similar athletes in the summer, or other available opportunities, take these. In all likelihood, you will encounter other athletes who are further along this timeline, and they can share some advice or experience that can help you along your journey.

I often get asked about how soon a family should start visiting a college. In terms of generating your (the athlete's) interest in a school, I think that 8th grade is about the earliest you should take college visits. These visits would NOT be linked to athletics, and I do not recommend trying to meet with coaches or promote yourself as a prospective student-athlete until you have established yourself as a varsity athlete.

Stage Two: 9th and 10th Grade

The priority in 9th and 10th Grade is to get off to a great academic start, while plugging in to your high school (or club) sports program. By the time you complete 10th grade, I strongly recommend making sure that you have earned at least 10 NCAA Core credits. This can include any Core credits that you accumulated during middle school. For any Core course that you receive a C or a D in, you will want to plan to take an elective in that category during your Junior or Senior year. While **getting good grades is the priority** during this phase, that should not come at the expense of continuing your athletic development.

This stage should also see you plug into an off-season training regimen. While my hope would be that your sport would have an in-season training plan, I realize that different programs and different schools vary on their in-season training philosophy. What should become a non-negotiable is the practice of having off-season physical (and sport specific) training become a habit. Talk to your high school coach about other opportunities to help you grow within the program and as an athlete. Lean into these without overextending yourself.

This stage is one where we want to function within your sport or sports as a varsity level or varsity bound athlete – and this involves social and physical skill development. As an athlete, you should become an advocate for yourself. Your parent(s) should be less involved as an advocate or a coach, and more involved as a supporter and as a fan. This should be seen in your building a relationship with your coach and your teammates, and to actively communicate with your coach on a regular basis.

Finally, I think that it is reasonable to visit colleges. If you have performed as a varsity athlete during 9th or 10th grade, then it might be appropriate to visit with coaches when you visit a school. However, before doing that, please talk to your high school coach to gage whether or not that would be appropriate. Whereas college coaches are extremely limited by their own rules in contacting you during this stage, they are free to talk to you if you go to them at their university. Just know that this alone will not make you a "recruit" for them, and there is a good chance that college coaches may be too busy to meet with you on a regular college tour visit.

Parents: please do not over-visit colleges during this stage. If there are schools that your player is interested in, I don't think it's a bad thing to visit these schools. You can visit them more than one time if practical. But please don't feel the need to go to a dozen schools during this stage.

Stage Three: Junior Year

Academically, this is a critical year. If you are a Division I prospect, you need to remember that you will have 10 core classes "locked" (7 of which are English, Math, and Science) at the end of your Junior year. Focus on making sure you are a **B- or Better** in all of your Core Courses.

If you want to play at the Division I or Division II level, register with the Eligibility Center at some point in time during your Junior year. If you do this before, that's perfectly fine. However, you should be registered before your junior year is over.

In the summer before your Junior Year, you should consider any camps, showcases, or tournaments that you might be able to use to demonstrate your talents to potential college coaches. If you have previously performed as a varsity athlete at your school, you may want to reach out to a college coach before attending a camp. We will talk more about how to handle camps and promoting yourself in the next chapter.

When you look at registering for your classes during your senior year, you should meet with your school counselor and determine your Core GPA. Decide how many Core Courses you need to take during your senior year, and build your schedule around that.

Finally, start expecting to "bump into" college coaches as they come to visit your school. The NCAA regulates the interaction they can have with you, so do not be offended if the conversation only lasts a few seconds or simply involves having information left behind for you to pick up. I strongly encourage you to be ready throughout both this stage and the next. Many of these visits are unscheduled and can catch you off-guard. Be at school, be in class, and look like a serious athlete or student. If you are at a school that does not get many visits from college coaches (usually due to location or school size), you can start to reach out to schools and coaches. Before doing this on your own, please consult your coach who can help guide you in the right direction.

Stage Four: The Summer Before Your Senior Year

This is a critical time period for you as a prospective student-athlete. To start, do whatever you can to come into this summer period in prime physical condition. Do not exacerbate injuries, and use the late spring to take care of any nagging injuries or ailments that can hinder your physical performance.

Work with your coach to outline a plan for attending summer camps, showcases, or tournaments. This will involve talking to college coaches, both yourself and your coach, as you plan your summer schedule. With your high school coach in on the planning, it is completely possible for you to be fully engaged with your high school team's summer activities and your own recruiting process obligations.

The summer is not simply about camps, tournaments, and

showcases. It should also be about visiting the colleges that have demonstrated a genuine interest in you. To determine "genuine interest" think about how often, and with how much interest, has a coach from a given college talked to you (this can include personal Twitter messages, texts, or emails). If communication was generic – meaning that it could have been or obviously was circulated to many people at once – then that particular college should not be a priority unless you think it is a top school in your mind. These visits are "unofficial visits" and the purpose is to get a feel for the college itself. Any interaction with members of the coaching staff is an added bonus.

If your primary sport is in the fall, I strongly recommend that you use the summer as best you can to promote yourself to college program. However, be ready to be all in when your high school season starts. There should be a distinct cutoff when you stop visiting colleges to focus on your high school season, especially since it is your senior season. If your sport does not start until the winter or the spring, you can continue your visits into the fall, but have a plan that will allow you to be fully present when your final season in high school starts.

Stage 5: Senior Year

During your senior year, the focus on your academics should continue, knowing which of your high school courses will count towards graduation and as an NCAA Core Course. This is not to suggest that you should slack off on your other courses, but more so to be vigilant to finish strong in the courses that can effect your eligibility.

This is the stage where you should be taking unofficial and official visits. I will explain the difference between an unofficial and an official visits in Chapter 11. These should be at the invitation of schools that are interested in you. In order to take any official visits to a Division I or Division II school, you will need to have created an account with the Eligibility Center.

This is also the stage where you should look to **narrow** your college choices. Go back through the answers to your questions in Chapter 1 as you evaluate colleges. Many recruits spend a lot of time and energy trying to get colleges to like/want them, that they forget that recruiting is a two-way street. Throughout the process you should be determining whether or not you want to attend a college. I strongly encourage you not to choose a college simply because they are the only one aggressively pursuing you. Yes, it is great to go where your wanted, but not at the cost of sacrificing your career goals, social aspirations, or other non-negotiable parameters.

In the process of narrowing, I have always encouraged my athletes that "we can consider other opportunities if they arrive but aren't on the radar right now." Until you sign a national letter of intent, you can change your mind. I strongly discourage this if you have entered into a verbal commitment to a school, and would advise you to be honest with your school if you intend to change your commitment. However, before committing or signing, you can both narrow your focus while being open to unknown opportunities that might arise. For example, a baseball player might narrow his focus to three Division II schools that have all offered him a scholarship and that fit what he is looking for. He can start to politely decline other invitations to focus on taking official visits to his three final schools. All the while, if a Division I school comes in with an offer (scholarship or PWO) before he has committed, he can evaluate that on a case by case basis.

This process is better than the converse situation, which I unfortunately see happen all of the time. This situation has a player hoping for a certain offer – either scholarship or level of play – and this hoping has left him or her neglecting other opportunities. Now, if the other opportunities go against your non-negotiables, then they aren't real opportunities anyway. However, to ignore opportunities because they aren't "good enough" at the time will often lead to disappointment if you try to go back to them at a later time and they are no longer available.

Stage 6: The Commitment & The Signing

I will outline the signing process and what you should be aware of in Chapter 12. The way this normally works is that you will decide on a school that you plan to attend. If this is a Division I or II school that is going to offer you an athletic scholarship, they will have a National Letter of Intent for you to sign during a specific window that the NCAA allows. The signing almost always follows the commitment phase.

A commitment is a stated decision to accept an offer at a particular school. This is not a binding commitment, meaning that either party – you as the athlete or the school – can back out of this at any time. While I strongly encourage my student-athletes to only commit after thought, prayer, evaluation, and family conversations that lead to a strong desire to attend and play for a school, one of the dark sides of recruiting is the number of times that offers and commitments are nothing more than lip service. I've had both things happen during my tenure – I have had an FCS school change their mind on one of my athletes days before the signing window opened, and I had an athlete bail on the school he committed to in favor of another school two days before he was supposed to sign. None of these are ideal situations, and they always arise because the circumstances have changed from the time of the offer and the commitment. So while you know that you can back out of your commitment, do not give a commitment flippantly.

Now, one of the harder parts of the recruiting process is this game of offer and commitment musical chairs. This process almost promotes distrust, yet all sides will say they want honesty and transparency. For you, the recruit, it is critically important to build a rapport with the coaches at the school you intend to commit to. They should feel as though you are already a member of their program, and you should hold the desire to be one. The coaches' jobs hinge on the ability to get commitments from the best athletes they can. If they have extended you an offer of any kind, they believe that you can help them win games and be successful at their level. When you commit to them, they are likely to move on from the others they have courted at your position or with your skill set. Likewise, they expect that you will cut off communication with other schools. If either of these is not true, then the offer should not have been extended nor accepted.

You might be thinking "yeah, but I've heard that _____ school has offered a lot of people." This is often the case, as coaches need to fill their recruiting class. This is another reason why you should build that relationship with the coaching staff if you want to solidify your spot. At the same time, they may have extended multiple offers out of the mindset that "we need 1 player at this position, so let's offer seven of similar ability, and we will be happy as long as we get one of them." This makes the offer time sensitive. I have seen this many times. It applies pressure to you, the athlete, but it's also the result of the coach not being able to fulfill all of their offers. Do not feel disrespected if a coach is pressuring you for a commitment once the offer has been made. There is nothing wrong with taking the necessary time to decide, but also understand that offers are not indefinite. Again, this is why the investigation, relationship building, and visiting campus when a mutual interest exists is so important.

When you decide to commit, and the commitment is reciprocated by your Division I or Division II school, this is when the Signing would take place. The NCAA holds certain windows that can differ by sport and age of the high school student-athlete, but your college of choice will work with you on when they expect you to sign.

Stage 7: The Transition

Chapter 13 will cover this transition in detail, and one of my main pieces of advice is to pour your energy into this Transition phase. For too many high school athletes, they see the Signing as and ending, when in reality it is a beginning. Your entire high school career should not be geared toward a 10 minute ceremony in which you sign a document that affords you the opportunity to continue playing. Your high school season culminated with the banquet after your senior season. The signing signifies a beginning of the next chapter in your playing (and academic) career.

Don't skip thinking about this stage in the process. Think about this stage while you are in Stages 5 and 6. If this stage is dreadful, then you will need to press pause on the recruiting process while you evaluate your desire and commitment to playing in college. If you are onboard with preparing and training to transition to college, make sure you design a transition plan. Some of this will come from your future college coach (possibly a strength training program, summer calendar opportunities after you graduate, etc.) and some can come from your prior experience. Plan the work, and then work the plan.

Final Thoughts

This timeline is a general reference, and it should give you some things to think about and/or do at different stages of this recruiting process. Remember, all of this centers around your involvement with your high school or club program. Colleges will eventually get to the point where they talk to your coach, and it is your coach's recommendation that will carry the most weight. Therefore, nothing outlined above should be done outside of your coach's awareness. In my experience, I am more than happy to help one of my student-athletes with recruiting opportunities, and if I have helped set them up, then I am accepting of any off-season conflicts. However, if a player operates outside of my awareness and misses team activities, that has a negative feel with both my coaching staff and my players (his teammates). Like most things in life, there is a right way and a wrong way to do things. Follow this general timeline and keep honest, open communication with all necessary parties. This will keep you on track and avoid conflicts. Finally, and I will say it again, be ALL IN with your high school development and experience. This commitment and focus will prepare you for the necessary mental framework to be successful in college, will give you the best senior season possible, and be an attractive quality to potential college coaches.

9 PROMOTING YOURSELF TO COLLEGE COACHES

The recruiting process is very similar to a dating courtship. To find the right fit, you need to be both actively representing yourself in the best way possible, while critically evaluating your potential options. There are a number of ways to present yourself in the best light possible.

This starts with your transcript. No, this does not mean that colleges are going to simply recruit the smartest kids. You have to be able to play your sport at a high level. However, your transcript is a starting point because there is a strong correlation between the maturity and habits that empower success in the classroom and the maturity and skills that will make you a successful college student-athlete. Prospects with good to excellent academic performance can be seen as an "added bonus" for a program. Different universities may incentivize their coaching staffs based on overall team academic performance, including grades and graduation rates. If you have a strong transcript, and therefore look to be a player to increase the team's GPA and be a future graduate, this is one advantage you may have over players with similar ability. Again, grades will not trump a perceived difference in talent or ability, but they can swing the decision in your favor if you are being weighed against others evaluated at a similar talent level.

Outside of the academic performance that shows on your transcript, there are four major avenues through which you can promote yourself: highlight film, leadership in your high school or club program, social media, and camps. This chapter will be spent outlining the "do's" and "don'ts" of these four areas. If your sport uses "showcases" instead of camps, much of the same guidance that I outline for camps can be applied to your situation.

In all of these areas, coaches are evaluating your ability to have a positive impact on their program. They care about the type of athletic ability you have – quite frankly, if you can't play on their team, they are not going to recruit you. But they are looking for much more than athletic talent. You might be the best player on your team, in your conference, in your region, and one of the best in your state. At the higher levels of play, coaches are evaluating anywhere from five to 50 players who are evaluated at a similar level to you. Stay humble and pay attention to how you present yourself. This will have a significant influence on whether a coach wants you in his or her program at the college level. They know their locker room, their roster, their school culture, and their needs better than you do, so their end goal is simple: will you fit in and make them better or not?

Highlight Film

For the college coach who evaluates over 100 potential recruits each year, the highlight film is often the "hook" that will move you onto their serious recruiting radar. There are right and wrong ways to put together a highlight film, and doing this the right way is critically important.

Highlight Film Do's:
- Place your name, school, accurate personal characteristics (height, weight, possibly times, and GPA) and contact information at the start of the highlight film
- Include your coach's name and contact information (either at the beginning or the end of the film)
- **Put your best plays at the start of the film**
- **Only use varsity game film** (No lower level, No Scrimmage film, No Practice film)
- Identify yourself clearly at the start of each clip
- Limit your highlight film to 3-5 minutes in length

- Cut out wasted time on each clip
- Use real speed (No slow motion, 1.5 speed film to look faster)

Highlight Film Don'ts:
- Don't put it together chronologically (game by game)
- Don't worry about setting it to music – coaches are not likely to listen with the sound on, and who is to say they like the same music as you do
- Don't put every play that you made all season long on it – keep it to 3-5 minutes in length
- Don't make a professionally choreographed video (training, drills, etc.)
- Don't put in slow developing clips that don't show your athleticism
- Don't include clips that show behavior that the coaches won't appreciate (if you got a taunting penalty after a big score, cut the clip before that is shown)
- Don't include inflated information – if you are 6 feet tall, don't list yourself as 6'2"

Your highlight film should always be looked at by your high school or club coach before you post it or distribute it to college coaches. If you want to post it on social media for friends and family members, that's perfectly fine. But if you want to use your highlight film for your one shot at getting a college coach's attention, make sure it is the best representation of your ability that you can put together.

Also, I mentioned not to make a professional choreographed video. What I mean by this is to avoid using an orchestrated production to promote yourself. Videos like this might look cool, and quite frankly be more interesting to watch, but they can be counter-productive in recruiting. The college coach will be skeptical about your ability if he/she feels that you thought you needed to dress up your highlights in order to be attractive as a recruit. Put your best varsity clips on film, and let your play speak for itself.

There are special situations in which you may need to produce an additional or supplementary video. As a coach, this may be something as simple as filming a lift, sprint, or agility drill during a team workout. Usually this is something that a specific coach has asked for, or an example to support a claim that I have made about an athlete while promoting him to a coach. For example, hip flexibility is an important question in evaluating football recruits, so I might film a player doing a parallel squat during a lifting workout and share that with an interested coach. Another time that this might be shared would be if a prospective student-athlete is recovering from a significant injury or a surgery. For example, if you are coming back from an ACL repair, it would be appropriate to make and share a video of you doing agility drills and sprinting once your recovery is complete. However, for athletes to simply make a "hype" video of a workout is not something that should generally be included in a highlight film.

Leadership in Your High School or Club Program

While I realize that many sports see recruiting happen through athletic teams that are not the high school team – AAU basketball, Club Soccer, Junior Olympic Volleyball, etc. – you also need to realize that there is a significant difference between these club teams and your high school team. I am not passing judgment that one is better than the other, but rather acknowledging that they are DIFFERENT. Your college experience will have strong similarities to playing on a high school team from the standpoint of having non-sport demands (academics), having some shared classes with your teammates, home facilities, a unified in-season and off-season training program, and the sense of community outside of your sport. This is one reason why I strongly encourage you to play on your high school team if possible. Yes, I have seen a handful of high school players who have not played on their high school team receive scholarship opportunities based on their club performance. However, if you go that route, I believe you lose access to a strong way to promote yourself through demonstrating leadership on your high school team.

High school teams have players from various backgrounds, often of different socioeconomic status, different talent levels (sometimes significant), and are significantly intertwined with academic rigors of being a student-athlete. Seeing you perform, both within your sport and outside of it, can give a college coach clarity about how you can translate to the college level. Can you show leadership on a club team? Of course you can, but those experiences are much more homogenous than high school teams, and your leadership that can be demonstrated is more clearly tied to playing your sport. Again, this is not knocking club athletic opportunities, but rather urging you to take advantage of the high school opportunities as well.

When it comes to leadership, especially to the college coach, **leadership is seen in action, not in title or awards**. Simply because you were named captain, or were an All-District athlete, this does not necessarily speak to your leadership. Captain voting can be a popularity contest or awarded because of a coach's preference, and performance awards are based on ability, not leadership.

A college coach will want to see how you lead – and you will lead if your sport is important enough to you to want to play it in college – by both observing you in different areas related to your high school team and in competition. How do you handle adversity? Leaders will come together and show grit in adversity, while others will isolate themselves or worse, assign blame. How do you interact with your teammates? Do they enjoy playing with you, or do you come across as a dictator? There's nothing wrong with calling the shots if that is your role. Leaders know how to connect, challenge, and encourage their teammates without sounding like a cheerleader or a dictator. Finally, how do you take coaching? When your coach challenges you, how do you respond? The best coaches will challenge their best players – do you lean into this and respond with intentional, positive effort? Or do you shrink away from it, assign blame, or make an excuse?

Think about these things. Far too many will quickly read over that, know what the right answer SHOULD be, and assume by default that they behave the right way. Here's the challenge: talk to your high school coach and some trusted teammates and ask them for honest feedback on these questions. When the college coach is watching from the stands, even if you don't know that he or she is present, I can promise you that they are evaluating these aspects of who you are. They are at your competition because they have already evaluated your talent as being able to play at their level… now they want to see if you have the intangible characteristics to make them better.

One thing to directly point out here is that **Leading By Example is Overrated**. Too many high school athletes claim that their leadership style is "leading by example" when in reality they are simply doing what they should do. Don't get me wrong, doing what you should do is a good thing, but this is a **base level expectation**. In college, if your coach says you have a workout at 6:00 am, the base expectation is that you will attend and participate with full effort. You aren't considered a leader because you show up. Leadership by example exists only when one's presence alone creates a change in behavior from others. For example, take a rookie player is drafted by the Lakers and shows up for a 6:00 am lift, only to realize that LeBron James has just finished a 90-minute basketball workout and is on his way to the same lift. LeBron doesn't have to say a word. The rookie will likely be in at 4:30 the next morning to do what the great ones do, simply because they have shown what it takes to be that great. This is a true leadership by example. However, I would also put forth that these great players – James, Michael Jordan, Tom Brady, Ray Lewis, Mike Trout, Alex Morgan – are also vocal, engaging leaders on their team. They would never just shrug their shoulders and say, "well, I lead by example, and that's about it." **Leadership is who you are as defined by your habits**.

So, what should this look like for you? Well, first and foremost it has to be **consistent**. You cannot lead sometimes. Second, it has to be **authentic**. Build relationships with your teammates and coaches, and build a trust that allows for challenges, persisting through adversity, and collective celebrations. Third, leaders do not expect things from their teammates that they are not willing to do themselves. Be on time – early is on time for a leader. Encourage your teammates, especially those who are new or might be disconnected, and do it in a specific, intentional way. The "Let's Go Guys!" rallying cry is both weak and hollow. **Leaders find a way to bring people together to win the moment**. If you aren't sure if you should speak up, speak directly and encourage people one on one. Simply raising your voice in a group is not leadership. Coaches want leaders, and you should want to be one. Therefore, to build your leadership, talk to your high school coach about things you can do to become a better leader.

As mentioned before, being a leader in your high school program should be consistent and authentic, but I also want you to be proactive in demonstrating your leadership when you know that a college coach is watching. When they come to watch you in a practice, game, or workout, or when they visit you at school, be aware that the little glimpses into your leadership and personality can be beneficial. Do you hustle from drill to drill? Do you encourage your teammates? Do you finish the drill? How do you interact with your coach? When they talk to you after practice, do you acknowledge your teammates by name? If they are meeting with you in the hallway, do you speak positively about your teammates, teachers, and coaches? Do you greet a friend by name as they pass you in the hall? Leaders aren't afraid to be coached, so how do you interact with the coach? Do you look them in the eye and provide non-verbal cues that you are interested? If you have a question for them, is it authentic? Think about these things. Don't panic and feel like you need to have some checklist whenever a coach is around, but rather be aware of the opportunities that present themselves to show your leadership and buy in to your collective experience (team, class, etc.).

Social Media

Social media is a modern day paradox. For so many, what is posted on social media elicits an emotional response and/or is the source of "truth" despite the veracity of what is posted. What I mean by this is that while social media is a 100% creative outlet, through which I can choose to present myself as anything I want to be seen as, yet it has no method through which to evaluate whether or not what I have created is real or imagined. So what's the point? The point is simple: **In a world where social media CAN present the best version of you, it becomes a double-edged sword that will either help or hurt your recruiting.** Not only what you post, what you like, and what you share, but how you frame it, all shed light on who YOU WANT PEOPLE TO THINK YOU ARE. For many, they have found social media to be an outlet of who they believe they really are. For the college coach, social media provides a glimpse into both: it shows both who you think you are, and what you must really be like. In addition, social media will be evaluated on what you choose not to post as well.

It is highly likely that by the time you read this, you have several social media accounts. While it is true that once you put something on the internet, it is never truly deleted, this does not mean that you should not try to clean up your accounts. At a shallow level, this sounds like deleting posts (tweets, snaps, pictures, etc.) that are inappropriate. But at a deeper level, I encourage you to think about (a) how do I want to present myself to college coaches, and (b) things that you think they are looking for in prospective athletes. Again, for many social media is a creative, passive-aggressive, thought sharing outlet, which is perfectly fine for them. If you want to use social media to help you in the recruiting process, you need to turn this outlet into an advocate for your aspirations.

Social Media Do's:
- Contain basic information you would want a college coach to have access to, and this can include your highlight film link
- Follow positive accounts and retweet or share positive posts
- Promote things associated with your team, teammates, and school
- Compliment your teammates and other athletes at your school in a respectful manner
- Follow college coaches that you have met or would like to meet
- Follow the accounts of the college teams that you are interested in joining
- Post positive, motivational materials
- Beware of things you like or share – even if you think the context is funny, college coaches might not understand or know the context
- Stay far away from accounts or posts that include extremely inappropriate language, racist or sexist content, or inappropriately violent content (a big hit in hockey is fine, but a sucker punch at a grocery store is not)
- Stay authentic – if you post or share posts about topics, make sure it is something you truly feel strongly about, and don't simply have a loose preference. Coaches cannot tell the level

of your commitment to the issue via social media, so only put your name on things you feel strongly about.
- Make sure your posts reflect your passion for your sport
- Post things that highlight your team, team events, and collective experience

Social Media Don'ts
- Do not post in an emotional moment, especially if it is a negative moment
- Do not post "inside jokes" that need context to explain that an outsider would not understand
- Do not post anything that compromises your moral character
- Do not post anything that promotes inappropriate behavior
- Do not post anything as factual without doing your research to make sure that it is actually factual
- **NEVER** throw your coaches or teammates under the bus on social media
- Do not over-promote yourself – if all of your posts are about yourself, and very few if any are about your team, you will come across as a narcissist or selfish player at best
- Do not create irrelevant media… There is a growing trend to share "hype videos" about oneself in a workout, or doing drills, etc. Whereas a clip of you nailing a max lift is appropriate, a choreographed, edited video set to music is not helpful
- Do not argue with anyone on social media – a fire without fuel burns out. Even if they attack you or your team. You might be arguing with a ghost. Don't show people that they can get under your skin on social media.

Again, I encourage you to remember what social media is and how it is used by college coaches. It is your opportunity to represent your "best self" to the outside world, and it is an avenue through which college coaches can get to know you. If they are looking at your social media accounts, they are already interested in you as a potential student-athlete at their school. You don't need to overhype yourself. Being a dedicated athlete who celebrates his team, teammates, and sport on social media will reinforce the positive attributes of what led them to look more closely at you in the first place. At the same time, if your social media portrays you as a hot-head, narcissist, inauthentic, or even worse as a racist, sexist, chauvinist, or sociopath, then this can cause them to move on from you as a prospect.

Use social media as a tool to promote the type of student-athlete that you are and that a college would want to join their program. I am not advocating that you step away from social media, just know its power and harness it for your benefit.

Camps

Camps give you, the student-athlete, the opportunity to perform your sport in front of the coaches who are recruiting you. In addition, it gives you the opportunity to experience the facilities at a college, and (in most cases) be coached by the coach with whom you will work if you play for that particular college. While each sport and the camps associated with the sport vary, I would strongly encourage you to talk with your high school coach about which camps are appropriate for you. This will make your time, travel, and monetary investment in attending camps the most worthwhile in the summers before your Junior and Senior year of high school. How to approach camps to get the most out of your experience and to best represent yourself through this interaction is important.

Once you have decided which camps to attend, I recommend that either you, your high school coach, or both reach out to a member of the coaching staff at the college and let them know of your plan to attend. If a coach has visited your school and met you, this should be the coach you reach out to. If you have not had contact, then reaching out to the position coach you are likely to work with is appropriate – let him or her know that you are excited for the chance to meet and work with them. Then, in the week leading up to camp, it is perfectly fine to mention on social media that you are excited for the camp and the chance to work with that staff, and I think it's fine to tag the coach in your post. If nothing else, you are helping them promote their camp.

On the day of the camp, be early. Not so early that you are weirdly eager, but early enough to check in and possibly have an initial greeting or conversation with a member of the staff (ideally the coach you will work with). Do what great athletes do – get a good night's sleep, hydrate and eat meals the day before and morning of that will propel your best performance, and make sure you have any clothing or equipment necessary for the camp. Be ready to go. This shows leadership and passion. Once the camp starts – be coachable. Be aware that some drills will be new, not just to you but to most campers, and tackle frustration and adversity with a positive attitude of persistence. **You don't have to be perfect at camp.** I encourage you to ask meaningful questions but not patronizing ones. Be engaged and build a positive rapport both with the coaches and your fellow campers. This shines a light on how you will be able to merge with your new teammates if you join their college program. When camp is over, take the time to thank the coaches you worked with. Don't be afraid to introduce a parent if they came to the camp with you. Parents: be courteous and grateful, but do not talk very much. And especially don't talk for or promote your own kid.

In the days following the camp, if you had a positive connection with the coach(es) that you worked with at camp, I recommend a simple follow up communication (made by you, the athlete). This can be a text, twitter message, or an email simply thanking them for their work with you during camp and noting that you enjoyed playing for them. Keep it simple. Don't be overly flattering but show that you are grateful. This is a small step, and not one that I would recommend if you don't take the time at camp to connect with a coach. But if you made the connection, this type of simple follow up can help you remain memorable to that coach.

Following these guidelines in the time leading up to camp, while you are at camp, and in the days following camp will help you put your best foot forward. If you are at camp with a lot of other campers, do not be discouraged. Many will fade into the crowd, which will give you the opportunity to stand out. Do what I recommended above. Make yourself memorable both for how you play and how you interact with the coach. Do not be discouraged by large camp numbers. When there are larger numbers, your performance can be accentuated if it stands out amidst a larger sample than being the "big fish in a small pond."

Some camps will have coaches from multiple schools present. Many times these coaches are from smaller schools or schools that don't compete with the host school for recruits. Treat all coaches with respect and interest. If you talk to a coach from a school that you haven't heard of, take the time to ask him or her about the school and the program. You never know where this coach will be coaching in the following weeks or months. Make a great impression on everyone. Who knows, maybe a school you had never considered will quickly become your top target. Don't worry about which college coach is talking to which athletes at a camp – put your best effort on display and make every interaction, with every coach and staff member, memorable.

Final Thoughts

Leadership, social media, and camps are all avenues through which you can appeal to college coaches. While recruiting is a two-way street in which you should be evaluating potential schools just as they are evaluating you, both parties should be putting their best self on display. Most of this chapter is highlighting the importance of being aware of what your best self looks like in each avenue, and then putting in the effort to utilize them to the best of your ability. There are many ways to move up on a recruiting board within a college program, but if you are crossed off a list, it is unlikely you will get back on it. Recruiting, from the college perspective, is the perpetual narrowing of the list of prospects. When you utilize these three methods of appealing to coaches, you position yourself to stay on lists as long as possible, provided you have the talent to succeed at their level.

10 COLLEGE VISITS

At some point in the recruiting process, you will need to get on campus and explore potential colleges and universities. Back in Chapter 1 you were asked to evaluate what you were looking for in a college, and visiting the college in person gives you the opportunity to start to feel out whether or not a school is a fit for you. Some families have been looking at various colleges from the time you were young. If this is your situation, if you liked a college years ago and want to consider it, I encourage you to go back for a more recent visit.

This chapter will cover four different types of visits: Off-Campus Visits, Prospective Student Visits, Unofficial Visits, and Official Visits.

Off-Campus Visits

This is the category that I classify when a college coach or college representative visits you at your high school or somewhere off-campus (not at the college itself). This covers a variety of interactions, with the most common being a coach swinging by your school. Depending upon your year in school, different NCAA rules apply to the type of interaction they can have with you. These interactions are often quick and are simply meant to make an introduction, express interest from both parties to get to know each other more, and to encourage opportunities to interact in the future.

My advice for these opportunities is to **be ready**. Be in class. Be at your workouts. Don't be late to practice. If this is a first impression, know that first impressions are powerful and can influence how a coach will view you as a prospect. These off-campus visits will not necessarily give you too much insight into the school itself or how it fits what you are looking for. One way to get some information would be to ask about the school size, majors offered, and anything important to you about the team (roster positions, etc.) Keep track of who you meet and follow up in an appropriate way. Some coaches will tell you "I'm going to follow you on Twitter, follow me back and I can message you." Follow through to start the recruiting relationship.

Off-campus visits will usually include an invitation to come check out a school. This is not a statement of being actively recruited, and it is likely afforded to every student-athlete the coach meets. However, if genuine interest on both parties, this is a starting point for which schools you should visit and/or plan to attend a camp.

Prospective Student Visits

This category of visit is when you visit a school regardless of your status of being a student-athlete at the school. These visits may or may not involve any interaction with members of the athletic department or your prospective sports team. A prospective student visit would usually involve a campus tour and an informational session from the admissions office. You should be able to see the dorms and cafeteria(s) and possibly even sit in and observe a class. This type of visit is not specifically set aside for athletes, as any prospective student can make this visit.

I strongly recommend that you do this. If there are schools that you know you hope to attend, you can do this before the recruiting process starts. If schools gain your interest after the recruiting process starts, I still think it is a good idea to take a visit that is not choreographed by the athletic department. This is not because I think that your sports team will present an inauthentic experience, but I think it only helps to have an independent evaluation of a school outside of the sports team (yes, even if the sport is your primary reason for attending the school).

When you are on a prospective student visit, come in with some questions that you would like the answer to in order to get a feel for the school. Only you can determine what these important questions might be, but put it this way, if it can influence your decision to attend or not, then ask. I also recommend this visit because it will give you the feel of being a student at the school if for some unforeseen reason you are unable to continue as a member of the athletic program. These visits often have tours given by current students, and they will answer questions directly and honestly.

Unofficial Visits

Technically speaking, the Prospective Student Visits, listed above would count as unofficial visits, but I separate the two because of the involvement of the sports program. An unofficial visit to a school is any visit you take at your own expense. This can be to talk to the coaches, attend a game on a "game visit", or to tour the school and facilities as being invited by the program you would play for. You can take an unofficial visit at your choosing or at the invitation of a college. There are no limits on unofficial visits to colleges.

Again, what makes it unofficial is that you make the visit at your own expense, and expenses incurred during the visit will be covered by you (or your family). This includes meals or other expenses. Colleges are allowed to issue complimentary game tickets to prospective student-athletes during unofficial visits. These visits are recorded by schools when you attend at their invitation. In addition, you need to know that simply receiving an "official game invite" does not mean that this is an official visit. As an unofficial visit, this means that if they serve a pregame meal, expect to have to pay for it.

Unofficial visits, especially for a game, can give you a great insight into the gameday atmosphere. Coaches will likely have only a few minutes to interact with you, because most of their time and energy needs to be focused on their game. You can get a great feel of the support of the student body, how the team interacts with each other, how the coaches interact with their players and each other during the game, and witness any gameday traditions. These are often fun experiences which can show the best of what the school has to offer within the realm of the competitive experience at their school.

Official Visits

Official visits are everything that the unofficial visits cannot be. This is the explicit courtship of a school to a student-athlete to try to sell the athlete and the family on the school and the athletic program of which you will be a part. In an official visit, a school will extend you an invitation for an official visit. The school is allowed to pay for all parts of the visit including meals, lodging, and travel expenses. This can include flying you and your parents across the country to visit the school, and it can include dinner at a fancy restaurant with the coaching staff. There will be tours, meetings with current players, possibly professors, and even admissions or academic counselors. Many times an official visit will result in you being paired with a current student-athlete at the school for an overnight visit. This will give you the opportunity to get to know some of the players on the team, see what the social life is like on campus, and get a feel for how you would fit in as a member of the team.

While many official visits will end with a scholarship offer being extended, some will not. If a school takes on the time and expense of paying for your visit, you know that they are genuinely interested in you as a prospective student-athlete. However, they are also recruiting other players at the same time. Each school handles this differently, but some may still offer an official visit if they do not have a scholarship to offer at that time. They would do this to generate interest on your end (as well to get to know you) should their situation change and an offer become available.

Remember, even if you are given an offer, and whether or not you choose to commit, nothing is binding until you sign a National Letter of Intent. Now, if a school has made the effort to bring you out for an official visit, it is likely that their scholarship offer is one that they have the intention of honoring. We will talk about the National Letter of Intent and Signing in Chapter 12.

Finally, the NCAA **only allows for up to FIVE official visits.** If you are fortunate enough to have multiple schools that are seriously considering you offer you an official visit, you need to know that these are not unlimited. In addition, many schools will host their official visits on the same weekend, both for efficiency and for giving you the opportunity to interact and bond with other players who may be joining you on the same team the following year. It is not unusual for a prospective student-athlete to make only one or two official visits. Schools are not likely to extend the invitation for an official visit unless they think you are seriously considering them as an option. **In order to take an official visit, you must have an account set up with the Eligibility Center.** The Eligibility Center will track your official visits. No school can offer you more than one official visit.

Final Thoughts

Visits are a critical part of the recruiting process. While I have seen a student-athlete choose a school without visiting, it was only due to extreme financial and logistical complications. So I strongly encourage you to get on campus more than once to get the "feel" for both the school and the sports team you would play on. As you go on visits, look for the things you want in a school, and compare what the school has to offer with the answers to your questions from Chapter 1. Ultimately, the right fit is more important than a certain level or scholarship offer, so knowing what you're looking for when you visit a school is of the utmost importance. It is easy to get swept up in the excitement of recruiting, especially when you are on a visit with other prospects. There's nothing wrong with leaning in to the excitement, but just set some time to critically evaluate what you have experienced while you are on campus to determine if it is the right fit for you.

11 RECRUITING VIOLATIONS

This will be the shortest chapter in this book, as there are pretty simple understandings for student-athletes and parents when it comes to Recruiting Violations. In recent years, there have been prominent violations that have hit the headlines. These are extreme cases and involve egregious violations of not just NCAA regulations, but federal law as well. My hope in this chapter will be to ease your concerns about accidentally coming in violation of NCAA rules.

Here's a rule of thumb: **Unless you request or receive money or items of significant value, you are not actively committing an NCAA violation.** The cases in the news have involved large sums of money being exchanged between private corporations, colleges (either with boosters or the coaches), in exchange for influence, access, and/or guiding top-ranked athletes into specific collegiate programs. If you pay for what equates to a bribe for your child to be recruited or admitted, or if you demand a bribe for your commitment to a school, these are violations. These are also blatant, intentional acts. You don't accidentally stumble into these situations. So rest easy, you will not run afoul of the NCAA rules during the recruiting process.

While the NCAA has received intense scrutiny and criticism over the years, the purpose of NCAA regulations is to protect you, the high school student-athlete from overbearing pressure from its member schools. The rules are in place to guide (or restrict) the actions of schools, coaches, alumni, and boosters as they relate to you as a prospective student-athlete. Before regulations were in place (or enforced) a top prospect could be called dozens of times a night by interested schools. Not only would this be stressful, but imagine trying to handle a high school season along with academic work when your phone won't stop ringing.

When it comes to talking to college coaches, know that when you – the player – initiate the conversation, that you are allowed to do this. If you call a college coach, I recommend that you do the following. If he or she answers, this is what you want. During the conversation, if you are going to call again, set up a time and date for the follow up. If you get the coach's voicemail, leave your name and basic information, along with a specific time that you are planning to call back. Then call back at that time – repeat this process if you get voicemail when you call back. I say this because the college coach might not be allowed to reach out to you, even calling you back, but you are allowed to reach out to them as much as you would like.

The only other area that you should be actively aware of is the **Amateurism** requirement to be able to participate in NCAA sports. As of the fall of 2019, legislation has been passed in California that has led to changes in the NCAA rules regarding the ability to profit off of your own image and likeness. This may change the understanding of Amateurism, and I encourage you to speak with your college coach or their athletic department counselors if questions about this come up. **To be safe, in order to remain an amateur, you cannot be paid or have received compensation for participating in your sport.** At least for now, if you have received compensation for playing your sport, the NCAA would consider this a violation of your amateur status.

Compensation can include benefits paid to you by a third party or an agent for future considerations. While only a tiny percentage of prospective college athletes (usually only blue chip, "sure thing" future professional athletes) would be exposed to an agent, just know that any third party that approaches you with benefits for you or your family could be problematic. In these situations, the most commonly reported (improper) benefits are "loans" to cover family travel expenses. They may also come offering connections to other opportunities outside of your sport, but make no mistake, this would be due to your athletic ability and popularity within the sport. In all likelihood, if you fit in this tiny realm of prospective athletes, your potential college coaches and their athletic departments will be vigilant in protecting you from being exploited by third parties. As a rule of thumb, if you are ever approached by a third party, make sure you run it by your college coach or athletic department before agreeing to meet or accept anything (including a free meal).

Final Thoughts

NCAA rules and regulations are in place to protect prospective student-athletes and their families. They do not expect you to know all of their rules, which is why they hold their member programs and coaches accountable to work within the rules. In order for you to be in violation, that would result in being individually penalized, you would need to have blatantly asked for or received impermissible benefits. This would take both you and your school (or it's representatives like boosters or alumni) or a third party agent to be actively involved with this type of wrongdoing. Don't spend time worrying about whether or not you are in compliance – you are in compliance outside of engaging in extreme action.

12 COMMITMENT, SIGNING, & THE NLI

The recruiting process will move into its final phases when you narrow your list of potential schools down to your top two or three, take your official visits, and see yourself playing at one above the others. Just as the school could "offer" you a place in their program at any point in time, you can "commit" at any time. This process will not be binding until you have signed a National Letter of Intent. The best analogy I can help to understand these stages is one of the dating/courtship to engagement to marriage. The start of the recruiting process is the courtship phase. You are gaging your interest in a school just as schools are getting to evaluate you as a potential member of their program.

When a school extends an "offer" you should seek come clarification about the level of their interest. Some schools will be vague – especially if they are a Division II (or FCS for football) – in the type and amount of a scholarship they plan to offer you. The question that you should ask upon receiving an offer is: "Is this a commitable offer?" What you are asking in this is, "If I commit to you right now, does that guarantee me a spot or scholarship or are you not that serious yet?" Don't be surprised if they aren't sure how to respond to that. Colleges – and even different sports within the same school – take different approaches to offers. Some offer early and often (I've seen an FBS school "offer" 200+ kids every spring) while others wait and only offer if they have a spot with your name on it. You won't know each school's approach, but asking the question above will help you get a picture of what they actually mean.

If an offer is not commitable at the time, this means that if you say "yes" or "I'm committing", they might not actually have a spot for you or offer you a scholarship at when the window for a binding relationship opens. However, if the coach tells you that it is commitable, that means that they have a scholarship spot for you on the roster and they are offering you the chance to join them. Most of the time this will come with a time stipulation. For example, a college basketball program might say something like, "Yes, it is a commitable offer. But to be fair, we have offered three point guards who fit our program, and we will only have a scholarship for one. So once one commits, then the offer will not be commitable for the other two." This will feel like a pressure play, when in reality it is simple honesty. Because you have asked the right question, they are saying that they truly want you, but that it probably won't last forever.

When you reach the point where you want to commit to a school, think of this like the engagement phase. The school has told you that they want you, have a spot and scholarship for you, and you want to take them up on it. When you commit, the school has prioritized you above other similar recruits, and in all likelihood will inform them that your commitment has reduced or eliminated possible opportunities for other recruits. This is simple math – if a school only has five scholarships to offer, and you are taking one of them, then there is less available for others. In addition, the school will likely expect you to behave the same way. This usually involves not taking any additional college visits, informing other college coaches of your decision, and a social media announcement. Both parties are indicating to other interested parties that they are focused on, and planning to, solidify their relationship when the signing window opens.

Before moving on to the signing, I want to urge you and your family to be fully aware of the commitment process before you commit to a school. Please determine the quality of the offer, and fully evaluate a school before committing to them. Keep in mind, nothing is binding during the engagement phase. You can commit to a school and later change your mind. A school can offer you and then later change their mind. The ideal situation does not involve wavering after a commitment, but it can happen. To avoid this, you must determine how committed a school is to you. How often are the coaches in contact? Does the head coach know your name? How detailed are they in talking about your future in the program?

Does it feel warm and welcoming or cold? Did they give you specifics about an offer, and do they have a planned official visit date? All of these will help you get a feel for where they stand on you – if they like you but aren't too excited, this could indicate that they will later change their offer. If they are very excited about you, the head coach and an assistant have been in your home, and have specifically outlined your role in the program, then you can have greater confidence in the offer. Likewise, I encourage you not to commit prematurely, even if you feel real or imagined pressure to do so. This does not mean that you should drag out the process or boast on social media about the offers you receive. When you feel connected and great about a school, and they have shown the same to you, this would be the time to commit and accept a commitable offer.

The wedding in this analogy is your "Signing" and this refers to the National Letter of Intent. Up to this point, the relationship is theoretical, no matter how serious one or both sides are. After you have signed the National Letter of Intent, the relationship is binding. This means that there are guarantees and penalties in place once you have signed. This locks in the commitment and the offer, resulting in membership within a college program.

Depending upon your sport, the NCAA has different time frames for when a Division I or Division II school can offer you a National Letter of Intent or NLI. The NLI is the formal document that formally binds a college and a student-athlete for the following year of participation in exchange for a scholarship. There are not National Letters of Intent, nor any binding document, for participation at the Division III level. While some student-athletes (or their families or schools) may mistakenly say that they have "signed" with a Division III school, this would simply be a ceremonially act and not an official NCAA agreement.

The amount of the scholarship will be stipulated within the NLI, as well as other stipulations that can make the agreement void should you show to be in violation. Some of the stipulations are to be expected – such as the requirement to graduate from high school and to be declared eligible by the NCAA Eligibility Center – and others may be unique to the school or the sport. For example, one softball player that I worked with received a NLI that stipulated that she could not "ski, ice skate, play hockey, or basketball" officially or recreationally after the signing of the NLI. Obviously this was in place to prevent injuries that could result from those activities.

The National Letter of Intent will have a short shelf life, with each having a specified expiration date. In all likelihood, if you are a Division I or Division II scholarship student-athlete, you will have chosen your school and "committed" to them before the window (for your sport) to sign a NLI. The coaches from your school will give you specific instructions on when and how to sign the NLI, and how to return it to them. Since the world of recruiting can be volatile and full of surprises, college coaches are most on edge when they have issued an NLI and are waiting for it to be signed. Therefore, you can expect them to ask you to sign it immediately when the window opens (i.e. 7:00 am – it will say it on the NLI) and get it to them right away (fax, email, text a picture). Once this has been done, you will need to return a signed copy to them in the mail.

One thing you will notice, is that this "signing" is procedural and not ceremonial. In the age of Social Media, the annual college signings for your sport seem to receive a larger amount of media attention. Even ESPN will cover the most prominent signing ceremonies for certain sports. Make no mistake, this ceremony is a show, and the actual NLI was signed and submitted as soon as the window opened. Unless you see a signing ceremony being broadcast live while you eat breakfast, it is very likely that the NLI paperwork was submitted early in the morning and the ceremony to re-create the "signing moment" for family, friends, teammates, and coaches is what you are seeing put out to the world.

What about Division III commitments?

As mentioned earlier, there is no National Letter of Intent to be signed to play at a Division III school because these schools cannot offer athletic scholarships. However, this does not mean that a commitment to a Division III school should be entered into lightly, nor with the intention of breaking that commitment should a scholarship opportunity arise. Before committing to a Division III school (or any school for that matter), you should evaluate and assess the school, and make decisions on how you feel about its role in your future academic and athletic development.

Division III coaches will work as hard as any in the recruiting world. Keep in mind, they have to sell you to not only want to play for their program and attend their university, but they also have to get you to want that so strongly that you are willing to pay for it. (Again, a majority of FCS and Division II scholarships are partial, so you will still be paying for some portion of your college costs). These coaches have recruiting boards, priority lists, rosters that need certain areas addressed, and competitive needs that they use in the recruiting process. Normally their reach is not as geographically expansive as some of the larger schools, but their schools may offer unique programs that can draw student-athletes from different parts of the country or world. When you commit to a Division III school, those coaches have offered you an opportunity to join their program in the same way that the Division I and Division II schools have. Respect that.

In my experience, one of the major (albeit superficial) drawbacks of student-athletes considering a Division III school is not being able to have a signing ceremony (since there is no NLI to sign). Some schools (players, parents, coaches) still hold a "signing" for Division III athletes and advertise it as such. This is disappointing to me. The end goal is not a signing ceremony, and I would encourage you to value your commitment without feeling the need to make it appear to be something that it's not. You should not have a "signing" ceremony when you are not signing. Instead, think about having an "announcement ceremony" or a "commitment ceremony" where you announce your commitment to a Division III school. You can have the same fanfare and "moment" that you desire, without the inaccurate effort to make it look like a binding agreement that occurs at the Division I or II level. Your teammates, coaches, parents, friends, teachers, and fans will be just as excited for you, and the ceremony will serve as a special memory as you publicly declare your commitment to continue your athletic journey at the collegiate level.

The Signing Ceremony

As alluded to previously, the signing ceremony is the public ceremony where you re-create the signing of your NLI for your family, friends, teammates, coaches, teachers, and fans to see. Each school, or possibly your high school program within the school, decides how and when to conduct a signing ceremony. If you are going to be offered one or more National Letters of Intent, and you want a signing ceremony to celebrate this moment, I encourage you to work with your head coach and Athletic or Activities Director at your school. They likely have a process through which they hold signing ceremonies, and it may involve having multiple athletes set to sign an NLI to have one collective ceremony. Whatever the process is, this is not something that you need to organize on your own. Tap into the people and resources in place to participate in a signing ceremony.

One note for you if you have a ceremony: think about what you want to say ahead of time. The signing ceremony will often allow a time for you to talk about your commitment, what drew you to the school, and other thoughts you have as you formally transfer your eligibility from high school to college. If you are more of an introvert, and speaking in front of a group is intimidating, I encourage you to write down your thoughts and simply read them aloud. This keeps you calm and on point. If you like speaking in front of groups of people, then do whatever is comfortable. However, I still recommend that athletes write down both the major points and the list of people they want to thank. This will prevent rambling that forgets to say what you really want to say.

Here is a broad outline as to what I recommend for your comments:
- Gratitudes (people to thank)
- Impact/Memories from high school (brief)
- What attracted you to make your college choice
- Thank people for attending

Finally, I strongly urge you to embrace the fact that your signing (or commitment) ceremony is a benchmark in your athletic journey up to this point. If it is an end point – if the goal of having a "signing ceremony" outweighs your desire to continue playing your sport – your career is likely in its final moments. Think of the signing as a starting point, rather than an end point. Runners don't celebrate a marathon when they announce their registration confirmation.

They celebrate the marathon when they cross the finish line. Whenever I speak to my athletes at these ceremonies, my final piece of advice is always "don't let this be the end, but rather the beginning of the next chapter. As hard as you have worked to get here... don't rest, continue to invest to make the next chapter all that you want it to be."

Final Thoughts

Throughout the recruiting process, you are aiming for it to end with the result that you hope for – connecting with a college opportunity that will facilitate your continued academic and athletic growth. The analogy of courtship, engagement, and the wedding can sound odd, but it can be extremely helpful when analyzing where you are at in the process with different schools. Do not commit before you are ready, and make sure that a school you want to commit to is also committed to you. Once you have committed, follow through. While the signing or commitment ceremony signifies the end of the recruiting process, your journey into collegiate athletics has just begun.

13 TRANSITIONING TO COLLEGE

From the start of this book, the purpose has been to help guide you – to provide some calm amidst the chaos – through the recruiting process. At some point, it will come to an end, and you will now be in a relationship with a college athletic program. The purpose of this chapter is to help you make as smooth of a transition as possible to the next level so that you will feel prepared, connected, and able to hit the ground running.

This all starts with your college program and your new coach. While they may have outlined the timeline for your transition to campus, I encourage you to ask questions and to start to develop a consistent and effective communication pattern with your coach. Here are the big questions you need to ask:

- When do I report to campus?
- Is there anything specific I need to know or do before I report?
- Should I attend an orientation session for new students?
- What are the living arrangements on campus?
- Is there a strength and conditioning program you want me to use?
- Are there events after I graduate that I can or should be a part of?
- Are there ways you recommend to connect with future teammates?

- What should I be asking that I don't know to ask? (ask this!!)

Your new college coach should be able to answer these questions, and the answers will help you feel both connected and informed as you transition to college.

Please do NOT just email all of these questions to your coach. First, look at the information that you have been provided after your commitment and/or signing. Some of the answers may have already been given to you. In that case, only ask clarifying questions. For example, if the information you receive says, "All incoming freshmen will report on August 1 at 9:00 am" please don't ask when to report. However, you might need to ask about which building to report to, what you need with you when you report, or possibly even a question about parking. But be sure to read the information provided before you ask the questions.

It is also just fine to ask the questions as the need for the answers becomes relevant. For example, if you commit in February, you might not need to ask the question about living arrangements until later in the spring. However, the question about ways to connect with future teammates is much more relevant as soon as you formalize your commitment. While you don't want to pester your coach on a daily basis, having some open and consistent communication in the time between your commitment and reporting to campus is recommended.

Along with gathering the information needed to be prepared to make the move (literally) from high school to college, I believe it is equally important to focus on developing the right mindset for the transition. When I have had players stop playing within their first few weeks of joining a college program, the most common reason is "it's so different from high school" usually masked in the "I lost the passion" statement. Well, it is different than high school because IT IS DIFFERENT than high school. If you prepare your mind for the transition, I believe you enter a new situation with your eyes open and the right attitude to be successful.

I am a firm believer that the most important part of getting your mindset right before joining the college ranks is to fully invest in a training regimen that will prepare you physically to be able to compete at the next level. This might sound counter-intuitive, but it is actually the most concrete action step you can take to prepare.

When you train your body, you are training your mind. After all, most athletes don't transition from middle school to high school with the expectation to be a varsity starter upon arrival. Yet many successful high school athletes become discouraged to find playing time limited or non-existent upon moving up a level. Thus, an intense physical training program will not only prepare you physically for competition upon arriving on campus, but it also trains your mind to understand the meritocracy of college sports – that is, you have to "earn" your role on the team, it won't just be given to you.

It is likely that your college coach will give you a training program for your off-season and the time between your high school season ending and when you report for training on campus. While each coach and program varies, one common theme is they want you to arrive in top physical shape. What I do NOT recommend is taking this program (usually a paper packet) and finding weight room time to work out on your own. The laziest workouts I witness each year come from seniors in high school doing "their own training" in order to prepare. There's rarely any accountability, no professional instruction, and this results in uncertain, low-intensity workouts. Make no mistake, when you get on campus, your coach is going to have you be all in with whatever the program's strength training program is (just like all other aspects of their program – study hall, eating, etc.) However, an uneducated, individual attempt to replicate that program off of a sheet of paper on your own is not a wise move.

Instead, I recommend finding a professional training outlet and working with those professionals to help you be physically prepared for your arrival on campus. If you take the training program given to you by your coach, the professionals can often utilize similar framework or movements in their work with you. I think there is great value in being challenged, driven, instructed, and if at all possible, working alongside other collegiate and/or professional athletes. If this is possible near where you live, even if it comes at a financial cost, I think it is a great investment in your future.

At my school, we have a very fortunate set up. We work with a professional training company called ETS. ETS has a proven track record of significantly developing high school, collegiate, and professional athletes. They provide our school's strength coach, and they do an incredible job working with our student-athletes. They also have multiple facilities across our state and in other states. Our student-athletes grow up training within their system, and we see incredible results. Some athletes at our school will seek additional training at the ETS facility outside of our team training in school. For those who become college-bound athletes, this is the outlet they use to continue their training between the end of their high school season and prior to their leaving to join their college program. In working with ETS, their experience is so comprehensive, that many will come back and work with ETS when they are home on breaks or over longer stretches when they are not involved in their college strength program. No matter what the long term set up looks like for each athlete, the fact that they have this program to plug into – to be challenged, receive coaching, and workout alongside other college athletes – prepares them to hit the ground running when they arrive on campus.

Please note: I am not advising that you hire a personal trainer. Often this is exactly what you should NOT do. This is not to devalue the work of all personal trainers. But personal trainers often have their own philosophies, training techniques, and end goals for their clients. If you want to train in a way that prepares you to be the best collegiate athlete you can be when you arrive on campus, you should train with the groups that train high level college athletes. I also believe in the power of collective training where you push, encourage, and compete with other athletes on the same journey as you are on.

Finally, get involved with your college team as soon as you are able to do so. The college coach knows the rules, so he/she can guide you on what opportunities exist. But be proactive in seeking out these opportunities. When you go on your official visit, get the contact information of those you interact with that will be on the team next year. Text, snap, like and follow on social media, and start to build a relationship with your teammates. If your college is geographically close enough that you can join them for some summer workouts before you report (this will have to be after you graduate from high school), participate when you can. Dive in. You are joining a new family and community, so the more ways you can plug in and become a part of it will be mutually beneficial.

And in this same thought process, it is perfectly normal and recommended to start to let go of superficial things that can hold you back. Be wary of who you hang out with from high school. Those who are not on the same mission as you will not have the same incentives to behave properly. Don't be afraid to use playing in college as an excuse to not do dumb things. Your "day one's" aren't really your friends if they want you to do things with them that can end your college career before it starts. Watch the news – it's unfortunate that we see this happen every year. If you aren't in a romantic relationship, don't start one in the months prior to going to college. Because of the inherent unknowns and insecurity that comes with leaving for college, many young people become MORE likely to start a relationship. While it might be true love, in all likelihood a new relationship is merely trying to hang on to the life you know. A relationship is not the end of the world… but when you're on campus at a place you've rarely been, with people you are just getting to know, the comfort of your new romantic interest will only serve to pull you away from being fully plugged in on campus.

Final Thoughts

Once you have formalized your commitment to play your sport in college, it is critically essential to prepare both your mind and body for the actual transition to college life and college athletics. Develop the proper mindset through training like you are starting at the bottom of the depth chart – in all likelihood, you are. **Be willing to grind**. Get with professionals who can help you be prepared when you arrive on campus, and try to work with other college-bound or current college athletes. Narrow your focus and stay on target. Allow things that used to be important but now have greater potential to hold you back, to fade into your history. If playing in college has been a dream of yours, it is now on the verge of become reality. **Pay the price to live your dream.**

EPILOGUE

This is an exciting and stressful time in your life. You have worked for years to hone your craft within your sport, put the effort into your academic studies to be successful, and recruiting can feel like staring into an abyss. Thanks for taking this journey with me through the recruiting process. My hope is that this practical guide can help you have some calm amidst the chaos; that you will know and be able to focus on what is important, and to ignore that which is not.

Remember, throughout this process your goal should be to find a college that you connect with, and one that will empower your continued academic and athletic growth. Know your non-negotiables and your desired components of a school, and focus your energy within those parameters. Avoid – **completely avoid** – the temptation to compare yourself to other athletes, especially those on your own teams that are on their own recruiting journey. Those comparative evaluations are worthless. Rather, encourage all of your teammates and celebrate their successes, especially within recruiting. Colleges are not choosing one teammate over another – they are making their own individual assessments. However, the more eyes on your team the better for all players with college aspirations.

Try to **have fun** in this process. It's a great chance to get to see different college campuses and to get to know different coaches and their staffs. You will meet other student-athletes going through the same thing you are. You will get to explore potential career fields, meet professors, experience various college gameday environments, and probably even get to know vibrantly supportive community members. This can be a fun experience. Ignore the "pressure" which is mostly a lie. Yes, you will eventually need to choose, but this is not a decision upon which the fate of the world lies. If after you decide on a school you determine that it was a disastrous decision, guess what? You can transfer to a different school. Yet, still don't make your commitment flippantly. But just know that the pressure is imagined or imposed (by people who are not you), so push it to the side and take it all in. You never know the course that your life will take, and it is quite possible for those who cross your path during this process to re-connect with you somewhere down the road of life.

I wish you the best of luck as you move through the recruiting process. Keep this book as a reference. Talk to your coach, both high school and college, and your school counselor if questions arise during your journey. Finally, never be afraid to chase your dream. **Don't expect an easy road, because every worthy cause travels through times of adversity.** Godspeed as you embark upon your path.

ABOUT THE AUTHOR

Andrew Hill is a Social Studies teacher and the Head Football Coach at Woodbury High School (MN) for the last nine years. He holds a BA in Secondary Education (University of St. Thomas) and a MA in Sports Science (United States Sports Academy). He has 15 years of head coaching experience, and 23 years of overall coaching experience. This has included working with football, boys and girls basketball, baseball, golf, and softball student-athletes. In addition to his head coaching position at Woodbury High School, he has served as the head football coach at Park View High School (VA), South Lakes High School (VA). The 2019-20 school year serves as his 20th as a classroom teacher. He has two children, Noah and Hannah, and two English Mastiffs.

Made in the USA
Monee, IL
19 January 2020

20525731R00069